MW01625104

CHASSIDIC LIGHT
IN THE SOVIET DARKNESS

by

Yechezkel Brod

arranged by

Menachem Brod

translated and adapted by

Daniel Goldberg

CHASSIDIC LIGHT IN THE SOVIET DARKNESS

Experiences of a Chassidic Youth in Communist Russia

by **Yechezkel Brod**

arranged by **Menachem Brod**

translated and adapted by **Daniel Goldberg**

Published and Copyrighted © 1999 by
Yechezkel Brod
424 Sterling Street, Brooklyn, New York 11225

For orders, please call:
"Mekor Hasforim" - (718) 627-4385
for out-of-State orders: 1-800-430-2067

All rights reserved.
No part of this publication may be reproduced in any form or by any means including photocopying and translation without permission in writing from the copyright holder.

Acknowledgments:
Yonah Avtzon for editorial suggestions
Yonason Hackner for copy-editing
Basha Majerczyk for editorial help
Moshe Weiss for layout and design

Printed in the U. S. A. By:
Moriah Offset Corp.
115 Empire Blvd. Brooklyn, N.Y. 11225, Tel: (718) 693-3800

DEDICATION

This book is dedicated to the eternal memory of two special personalities who left an indelible impression upon me:

My grandfather Reb Naftoli Hertz Nachlis,
murdered by the accursed Nazis on Yom Kippur, 1941.

Rabbi Aryeh Leib Kaplan,
also murdered by the accursed Nazis on Yom Kippur, 1941.

May G-d avenge their blood, and may their pure characters illuminate our path.

IN ETERNAL MEMORY

On 28 Shvat, 5756, my older sister Reizel Estulin, of blessed memory, passed away and was laid to rest in Jerusalem. Her life was one long chain of true Mesiras Nefesh for traditional Jewish education. Despite the frightful personal danger, she gladly allowed her home to be used as a branch of Yeshivas Tomchei Tmimim, and raised her children to Torah study, fear of G-d, and devotion to the Rebbe. After reaching the Holy Land, she would go every Friday, on the Rebbe's instructions, to hospitals to encourage Jewish women and girls to light Shabbos candles.

Mrs.Reizel Estulin receives the Rebbe's blessing

CONTENTS

ב"ה

PREFACE

Chassidus emphasizes humility. In fact, it is so fundamental to Chassidus that, for anyone aspiring to be a Chossid, the very idea of publishing a book about one's personal experiences, however interesting, seems somehow out of place.

Nevertheless, Rabbi Yosef Yitzchok Schneersohn (1880-1950), the sixth great Rebbe of Chabad-Lubavitch, and also his celebrated son-in-law, our own Rebbe, often directed Chassidim to commit to writing their oral traditions of the history and anecdotal material of our great Rebbes and Chassidim of past generations, and also of their experiences in the struggle to preserve Yiddishkeit in the Soviet Union.

However, never would I have dreamed that that directive applied to me. True, I had many extraordinary experiences under the Soviet regime. But in that respect I was no better than thousands of other Chassidim, many of whom endured tribulations far worse than mine, especially those who were tortured in Soviet jails and suffered for years in hard-labor camps for teaching Torah or even just for being observant Jews.

Never would it have occurred to me to write my own life story, nor was it in my nature, if not for an utterly unexpected visit I had in the early years after I settled in New York: My visitor was Dr. Nissan Mindel, one of our Rebbe's respected secretaries. Among his many duties, he edited two children's magazines, "Shmuessen mit Kinder un Yugend" in Yiddish and "Talks and Tales" in English. Dr. Mindel told me that the Rebbe had suggested he write up some of my experiences in those magazines!

I was astonished. At that time, I was under constant pressure just trying to support my young family. The many refugees reaching these shores after World War II were finding that settling down here was far from easy. Not only was the language new; even harder were the vastly different ways of this land. Finding employment was hard, especially for Shabbos observers, and available jobs usually were low-paying and required working long hours.

Under such circumstances, publishing memoirs was the furthest thing from my mind. It would seem more appropriate to put it off for my later years, after "making it" in America.

Naturally, of course, since the initiative came from the Rebbe, I agreed to Dr. Mindel's request. However, to protect my family members and others still in the Soviet Union, I insisted that my name and certain facts be changed. Although we were so far away, we still had reason to fear the long Soviet arm for reprisals even against us (several incidents over the years have brought home to us that the worldwide Soviet intelligence network was aware of everything happening among Soviet emigres here and in Israel, down to minor details!). Certainly this was true for those still fully at the regime's mercy.

Therefore, when my story was published - first in Yiddish in the "Shmuessen," and later in English in the "Talks and Tales" - the "hero's" name was changed from Yechezkel to "Mendel"!

Only now, after the fall of Communism and the

disintegration of the Soviet Union, do I feel free to tell the story of my life there exactly as it happened. That explains why certain details here differ from the story as published in those magazines. Finally the time has arrived when I am able to fully do what the Rebbe wanted. Every detail in this book as now published is the exact truth the way it happened. Any detail of which I was unsure I preferred to omit rather than write something that may not be true.

Another reason for publishing my life story is to bequeath to my children and grandchildren my "legacy." They must be aware of how pious Jews and Chassidim, including their own ancestors, lived lives of amazing sacrifice under the harshest conditions, in order to remain true to G-d and His Torah, to keep Shabbos, and to ensure that their children learn to live and die as Jews.

During those years we became accustomed to enduring hunger, cold and fear. During my early childhood, I would often go to sleep hungry, wake up hungry, and go hungry all day. Both at home and during my wanderings to learn Torah, the buildings where we lived and slept were often unheated; I would curl up in my thin coat in a vain attempt to withstand the biting cold of the Russian winter.

Worst of all was the incessant fear that gripped everyone. If we ventured outside, we would constantly cast furtive glances all around for fear of being followed. While we studied Torah in secret, we knew that at any moment the dreaded knock at the door might come and off we would be dragged to jail and worse...

Thank G-d, here in the United States we suffer from none of these. We are free to keep the Torah without restraint, and American society even encourages and helps us to observe it.

Although I have had difficult experiences here, too, my purpose in this book is not to tell of my life in the United States but to describe some of the Mesiras Nefesh (self-sacrifice) for Yiddishkeit that my parents and many other fine Jews had during that difficult era.

May G-d grant that the merit of our holy ancestors and parents who gave their lives for G-d and His Torah - some literally and others who were prepared to do so at any moment - may protect my wife, myself and all our descendants until the end of all time, materially and spiritually, and that we be privileged to witness the revelation of Moshiach, may it be very soon!

* * *

It is my pleasant duty to express deep gratitude to my nephew Menachem Brod for his generous investment of time in arranging, editing and publishing this book in its Hebrew version, including the gathering of appropriate pictures. I also thank my son-in-law, Rabbi Moshe Yosef Weiss, and my sons and daughters who all contributed in various ways to preparing the original book for publication. Special thanks go to my daughter-in-law, Freidy Brod, for preparing the index of names and places in the Hebrew version.

May they all be repaid by the Almighty, for Whose bounty in preserving me and my family I give thanks daily.

10 Shvat, 5759

Yechezkel Brod

TRANSLATOR'S NOTE

In recent years, several books have appeared that chronicle the heroism of Jews to maintain Yiddishkeit in the face of Soviet persecution. This book, however, is unique in being the first to portray events through the eyes of a Jewish boy growing up in a Torah-observant family under the incredibly difficult conditions of the time.

Besides suffering the travails of hunger, cold and fear that affected most other Soviet citizens, too, the author had some extraordinary experiences that reflect the reality of life under the totalitarian Soviet regime. Describing them in book form is not only a service to historians of the era but also an invaluable contribution to the education of today's youth, who often have little idea of the heroism Jews have had in the recent past to observe Yiddishkeit and maintain their children's identity as Jews.

Reading through the author's dramatic account enables us to "relive" that awesome era when all hope seemed lost for the future of Yiddishkeit. By comparing it with our own era, when Yiddishkeit has risen miraculously like a phoenix from the flames of Soviet persecution, the Holocaust, and worldwide assimilation - mainly through the toil, example and encouragement of our Rebbe - we can appreciate how significant is our present era of preparation for the revelation of Moshiach, may it be very soon.

Translating this book has been an exciting experience for me, and I hope the readers will feel the same sense of excitement as they follow the author's dramatic life story.

Daniel Goldberg

CHAPTER ONE

EARLY MEMORIES

FATHER'S FAMILY

My parents were from two sides of the Russian-Polish border.

My father, Reb Chayim Binyomin Brod, of blessed memory, was born in Poland. He was just four years old when his father Reb Yechezkel (after whom I am named) passed away.

His widowed mother was left with the burden of supporting Father and his two sisters, and of paying for his Torah schooling at Cheder. She started working for a living. Then came another blow. Not long after she began work, she had a serious accident.

Both her legs were broken and her whole body was injured. For many months, she was forced to rest in bed before she recovered, intensifying the family's poverty even more.

Years later, my grandmother was still so poor that when

her daughters reached marriageable age she had no money to marry them off. One day a Jew selling lottery tickets knocked at her door. He insisted that she buy one, refusir to hear any excuses that she could not afford it. He simply would not leave until she bought one. That ticket brought her good fortune: With G-d's help, she won the lottery with enough money to pay for both her daughters' weddings, and plenty left over to support her in the future!

FATHER GOES TO UMAN

Around the age of eighteen, Father happened to read some writings of the Breslov Chassidic sect. He was so impressed that soon he joined the group of Breslover Chassidim in his town.

Breslover Chassidim consider it highly meritorious to visit the grave in Uman of their renowned founder Rabbi Nachman of Breslov (1772-1810), great-grandson of the Baal Shem Tov. But Uman is in the Ukraine, which was under Russian rule.

At that time, during and after World War I, hostilities continued sporadically and borders were changing. But Father and nine of his companions yearned to go to Uman. Without telling their families, they found a way to cross the border to reach their destination.

From Uman, Father wrote to his mother not to worry as he would soon return home. "Many are the thoughts in the heart of man, but it is G-d's plan that endures" (Mishlei 19:21). Not long after they arrived, the Soviets closed the border permanently and the ten young men, including

My parents, Reb Chayim Binyomin Brod and Mrs. Shlima Rivka Brod, after their arrival in the Holy Land

Father, were forced to stay in Russia.

MOTHER'S FAMILY

From Uman, Father went to Mezibuzh, which was closer to the Polish border. The town is so small that many maps of Ukraine don't even show it. But among Jews it is famous as the center of the holy Rabbi Yisroel Baal Shem Tov (1698-1760), founder of Chassidism, during his years as leader of the movement.

While Father was in Mezibuzh, a match was arranged for him with my mother, Shlima Rivka, of blessed memory. She was her parents' only child and her father, Reb Naftoli Hertz Nachlis who was from an old Mezibuzh family descended from the renowned Rabbi Shimshon of Ostropoli – had given her her unusual first name in memory of his own father Shlomo.

Rabbi Shimshon (ca. 1600-1648), one of the greatest Kabbalists, was a grandson of Rabbi Shimshon, Rabbi of Kremnitz, son-in-law of Rabbi Betzalel, brother of the renowned MaHaRaL (Rabbi Yehuda Liva-Loewe) of Prague. As inscribed on Rabbi Shimshon's tombstone, he was among three hundred Jews murdered in Polonoy on 3 Menachem Av, 1648, during the cruel Cossack massacres led by the accursed Bogdan Chmielnicki, when hundreds of thousands of Jews were slaughtered.

My grandfather Reb Naftoli Hertz was also murdered, together with all the Jews of Mezibuzh, on Yom Kippur 1941. The accursed Nazis forced the Jews into the fields outside the town where they mowed them down with their guns. One girl fell unconscious, wounded by their bullets, and was left for dead. During the night she recovered consciousness and escaped, reporting the gruesome fate of her townsfolk – the fate of most of Europe's Jews – to other Jews.

May G-d avenge their blood!

"G-D WILL PROVIDE..."

At my parents' engagement party, my grandfather asked Father how he intended to make a living. Before he had a chance to reply, Father's companions started singing a song to the words "He [G-d] provides sustenance, He gives livelihood..." – effectively closing the subject!

(This incident was related to me years later by Rabbi Moshe Bick, one of Father's companions who was present then. Later he moved to Brooklyn, New York, where I made

Rabbi Chayim Bick, of Mezibuzh and New York

Rabbi Moshe Bick, one of my father's friends

his acquaintance. He was a well-known Rabbi and also a Rosh Yeshiva at Yeshivas Chasan Sofer. Here I met his father, too, Rabbi Chayim Bick, originally of Mezibuzh and also a well-known Rabbi, whom I would visit often. One winter when he was sick at Beth Israel Hospital, I spent many long evenings listening to his interesting narratives.)

WORK ON SHABBOS OR STARVE!

My parents were married not long after the 1917 Bolshevik Revolution. The new regime exerted its hold over the land by appointing Communists to every town's key positions and prohibiting any business or independent occupation.

As a small town, Mezibuzh had limited opportunities for livelihood. The Jewish Communists who now controlled the town were determined to stamp out Jewish observance. Whoever needed a job had to apply to them. They had just one condition for granting a job: Work on Shabbòs!

Right after his wedding, Father discovered that he had to make a bitter choice – either work on Shabbos or starve! Naturally, he refused to work on Shabbos.

"Just wait!" the Communist officials told him. "It won't be long before you'll be back in tears, pleading with us to give you work, Shabbos or no Shabbos!"

But Father remained resolute. "Under no circumstances will I ever work on Shabbos!"

His decision meant, in effect, condemning his family to constant hunger. My older sister Reizel, of blessed memory (later to marry Reb Zalman Leib Estulin, who now lives in Bnei Brak, Israel), was born in 1920, and I was born on 25 Nissan, 1923.

During our childhood, we often starved.

One incident I remember illustrates our grinding poverty:

Once, when I was about six, I accompanied Father to Shul on Shabbos morning. We returned home to find our table empty of food. We had hoped for at least a piece of bread on which to make Kiddush and still our hunger (wine for Kiddush wasn't even something to dream of). But there was absolutely no food in the house.

With his typically Chassidic attitude, Father tried to look at the situation positively. With a smile he told us that "Shabbos" in Hebrew is spelled with three letters, which can stand for the three words "Sheina B'Shabbos Taanug" – on Shabbos, sleep is pleasurable.

"When there's nothing to eat," he said, "we can enjoy Shabbos by taking a nap!"

My stomach groaned with hunger pangs. As difficult as

it was, I finally dozed off. Soon after midday I awoke and noticed a piece of bread on the table. Asking no questions, I gobbled it down hungrily. Apparently a neighbor had discovered that we had nothing to eat and brought us in some bread...

IMMERSION UNDER THE ICE

Many are my fond memories of Mezibuzh. During my years there, I was privileged to pray in the Baal Shem Tov's Shul. On Simchas Torah, I was privileged to participate with the other children in the "Kol Han'orim" Aliya read out of the same Sefer Torah scroll reputedly read for the Baal Shem Tov's own Aliyos to the Torah.

My grandfather told me much about the town's history, and described striking personalities who had lived or visited there.

Once he told me how amazed he had been by a wayfarer – apparently a Chabad Chossid – who passed through Mezibuzh one winter. With an axe he had broken a hole in the ice over the river to immerse himself in preparation for prayer. From the icy river, the Chossid went to pray in our town's "Cold Shul" – so called because its large size made it suitable for use mainly on the High Holidays, while it stood empty and unheated most of the year. The Chossid spent many hours in prayer in that cold building, yet emerged later covered in sweat as if coming out of a steam bath!

The holy resting place of Rabbi Yisroel Baal Shem Tov in Mezibuzh

AN HONORED GUEST

Father became very close with the renowned Chabad Chossid Rabbi Yitzchok Hurvitz, known as "Reb Itche the Masmid." Once, when Reb Itche came to pray at the Baal Shem Tov's grave, Father invited him to stay with us. Reb Itche accepted, but gave Mother special instructions for preparing his food, as he had unique personal stringencies in observing Mitzvos, especially in Kashrus.

On Shabbos, the town's Jews thronged to watch Reb Itche's fervent prayer that lasted most of the day. Never had they seen such heartfelt prayer with such sweet outpouring of the soul in utter devotion to G-d...

Rabbi Yitzchok Hurvitz, known as "Reb Itche the Masmid"

Father asked Reb Itche to give me his blessing. Placing his hands on my head, Reb Itche gave me his blessing to grow up a G-d-fearing Jew. A few years later, when I joined Father briefly in Moscow, he asked Reb Itche to bless me again. Thus I was privileged to be blessed by him twice.

Many years later, in 1970, after Father had left the USSR and settled in the Holy Land, my nephew

Naftoli Estulin became engaged to Reb Itche's granddaughter Feige (youngest daughter of his son Reb Tzemach Gurevitch, now living in Crown Heights, Brooklyn).

Father was beside himself with emotion: "How do I deserve this great privilege that my grandson is marrying Reb Itche's granddaughter?" He decided it must have been in the merit of serving Reb Itche so devotedly when he was a guest in our home.

FATHER FLEES

Besides the difficulty of earning a living, the Communist authorities suspected Father of being a religious activist, which was prohibited. Although he tried to remain unobtrusive, when he realized that they had an eye out for him, he decided to escape town. Mother was left with the burden of supporting the family.

Sometimes Father would send her some money, but the family's economic situation worsened.

Eventually Father realized that in Mezibuzh the authorities would never leave him alone. Anyway, there was little chance of making a living there. Uman, on the other hand, was a larger town where he had many friends. He felt he could more easily find work there that would allow him to keep Shabbos without being noticed by the authorities. In 1931, my parents decided to move to Uman.

CHAPTER TWO

MY PARENTS' LEGACY

MESIRAS NEFESH

Those fortunate to be born in the free world find it difficult to appreciate how hard life was for our parents and grandparents in Russia, and how much they sacrificed to raise their children as Torah-observant Jews. My parents were an outstanding example.

Father was a unique personality. Unfortunately, the years that I spent in his company were relatively few. During my childhood, he often had to leave home and stay in faraway places. As I grew older, I too left home to study at Yeshivos, wandering far and wide through the Soviet Union. But the time I was privileged to spend with Father I will never forget.

GROANS OF JOY

My parents had little material reason to be happy. Their grinding poverty and lack of basic necessities, besides the nagging worry about their childrens' future identity as Jews and the constant fear of government persecution, among so many other concerns for simple survival, were enough to make anyone forget about joy and happiness.

Regardless of all this, however, Father was always bubbling over with irrepressible joy and enthusiasm. I remember how once, while Father lay ill in bed, drained of strength, some friends came over to fulfill the Torah duty of visiting the sick. Their visit gave him new energy, and he jumped out of bed to dance with them around the room!

Father often sang, especially when he was hungry – which happened frequently – to divert his mind from the hunger. Once, when I was six or seven, I noticed that while he sang, he was swaying from side to side with strangely sharp movements. When I asked him why, he told me he had a bad toothache.

"So why are you singing?" I asked.

"When someone has a toothache," Father explained, "he groans.

"I'm groaning, too. But my groans are groans of joy! It's bad enough that I'm in pain myself. Why make everyone else feel bad, too?"

Mother once asked him how he could be so happy when they had so many worries. Father replied: "You know how weak my body is. I don't have the strength to bear even a tenth of our worries. So let's find some gentile ruffian to carry all my worries for me..."

SPEAKING DIRECTLY TO G-D

Father paid special attention to my Jewish education. Until my brother Yisroel was born after my Bar-Mitzva, I was his only son, and Father spent as much time with me as he could. When we lived in Mezibuzh, he told me of the many great personalities who had lived there: the Baal Shem Tov, and his famous grandsons, Rabbi Moshe Chayim Efrayim, the Rabbi of Sadilkov (1748-1800), author of "Degel Machanei Efrayim," and his brother Rabbi Boruch of Mezibuzh (1753-1812); Rabbi Avrohom Yehoshua Heschel (1755-1825), renowned as the Apter Rov and author of "Ohev Yisroel," and many others.

He made sure I understood the deep significance of the times:

The godless Communists had seized the land and were persecuting Jewish observance. Unfortunately, many of them were Jewish themselves. Father worked hard to implant in me the conviction that the Torah and Mitzvos are the only true path. Accordingly, we had to be ready to give our very lives for Torah education and observance of Shabbos, Kashrus and the other Mitzvos.

A fundamental point Father emphasized was that G-d considers every Jew as His only child. Every Jew can therefore always approach Him as a child approaches his parents. It is the nature of a child that, when he has a problem, he runs to his parents for help. Sometimes he runs to them quietly, sometimes noisily, sometimes in tears. And his parents always understand what he wants.

"You're starting life in this world," Father told me, "and

The Red Army entering a Russian city

you see the conditions we are living under. Whatever happens to you, remember that you can always approach G-d and ask Him for your needs as a child asks his parents. If ever you are in danger, mention your name and your mother's name and beg G-d to save you."

Those words penetrated deeply into my heart. Over the years, that advice came in handy. There were times when I was literally in danger of my life. I followed Father's advice and, with G-d's help, was always saved.

MITZVA ACTIVISM

Although it was highly dangerous in the USSR, Father was active in what we call today "Mitzva Campaigns." Whenever he met a Jew, he would ask him whether he kept kosher, had Mezuzos on his door posts, and donned Tefilin every day. He was overjoyed when he got a Jew to put on

Tefilin, and his face shone as he helped him wrap the straps around his arm and head.

When Father had to leave home, he lived for several years in Moscow. Sometimes he would travel from one end of that huge city to the other to buy a chicken, have it ritually slaughtered by a Shochet, and bring it to a Jewish family so that their kitchen could stay or become kosher. He devoted boundless energy to such deeds.

In later years, despite the ever-present danger, Father devoted himself totally to these activities, raising funds to buy Tefilin, Tzitzis, prayer-books and traveling to distant parts of the USSR where he would encourage Jews to don Tefilin, wear Tzitzis and pray daily, among other Mitzvos. If they could afford it he would ask them to pay the cost, while those in need would receive the Tefilin as a gift together with financial assistance.

FATHER'S HEART OF GOLD

It was his deep love for other Jews that made Father want to help them keep Mitzvos. For Father had a heart of gold. We often hear the words "Ahavas Yisroel" - love of fellow Jews - these days.

But in Father I saw its true meaning. When it came to helping another Jew, nothing could get in his way, and he would give everything, even endanger his life, to do a Jew a favor.

Sometimes Father's kindness reached levels that amazed even his own family, for he was willing to give up basic family necessities to help another Jew. Many examples engraved in my mind:

In Uman lived a Breslover Chossid named Reb Dovid Geisinsky.

Although it was strictly forbidden by the government, at risk of the worst punishment, Reb Dovid ran a successful fur business and made a fortune.

To show how much his economic situation was better then ours: When his son Bentzion – a friend of mine who studied at the same Cheder, though he was older than I – once invited me home for Shalosh Seudos (the third Shabbos meal, eaten in the afternoon), I was amazed to see how much food adorned their table. Never had I seen so much food before!

In our home, a piece of bread and some cooked dish would be considered a royal banquet! All week we thought ourselves lucky to have even such simple food as beans. For Shabbos, we didn't dream of meat or chicken; the only special food we could ever afford was small fish, which were sold very cheaply because few people were willing to bother with the lengthy preparation they required.

One Friday evening, on our way home from Shul, Reb Dovid mentioned in the course of conversation that his family had no fish that Shabbos. His wife had wanted to buy a large fish, but a non-Jew had offered much more money and bought it. She did not care to bother with small fish because they required too much work. So they had no fish that Shabbos.

The conversation shifted to other subjects. When we came to our house, Father asked Reb Dovid's little son

Yankele to step inside with us for a moment, apparently without Reb Dovid noticing.

After wishing Mother "Good Shabbos!" he took Yankele into the kitchen, then quickly sent him home.

We sang "Sholom Aleichem," greeting the angels who had accompanied us home from Shul. We washed our hands and Father made Kiddush on the bread. Then Mother went into the kitchen to bring in the fish.

Mother had stayed up late on Thursday night to clean these finger-sized fish, spending many hours separating the tiny scraps of fish from the skin and bones, then grinding them and adding flavoring before cooking. But the precious fish had disappeared!

Mother came back in and looked at Father questioningly.

In a low voice, Father explained that Reb Dovid had mentioned that they had no fish for Shabbos, so he had asked little Yankele to take the pot home.

Mother was heartbroken.

"You're right!" she managed to say. "Certainly we have to help another Jew. But surely Reb Dovid doesn't need your help. His table has plenty of food on it, without our fish."

"But we are used to doing without food," explained Father.

"Sometimes we have what to eat, and sometimes we don't. If we do without fish one Shabbos, our Shabbos won't be disturbed. But Reb Dovid's family isn't used to a Shabbos without eating fish. It would detract from their Shabbos joy to go without it..."

SELF-SACRIFICE FOR OTHER JEWS

In 1933, Father went to Moscow to look for work. He found a job as a night watchman in a factory. This was extraordinarily good luck, for his job was to keep watch inside the building, which was warm and comfortable. Besides employment, he had a roof over his head at night, and a quiet place to study Torah and pray.

At that time, citizens streamed to Moscow from all over the USSR, among them many Torah-observant Jews. Some were fleeing possible arrest, while others sought livelihood in time of famine (during the early 1930's, the regime created a famine in order to crush the independent-minded Russian peasants). Others were there to apply at government offices for exit permits, which were still granted occasionally.

For food, these Jews could always buy bread or unprocessed foods. But a place to stay overnight was a big problem. Officially, anyone arriving in a new location had to register with the local government. It was prohibited to let anyone sleep overnight at one's home without notifying the block supervisor, a government agent. No one could be blamed for being unwilling to endanger himself by taking in guests. Besides, few people had space in their homes for guests, as most lived in just a room or two, sharing apartments with other families who were usually non-Jewish or anti-religious and might report a guest's presence to the authorities.

When some of these Jews heard that Father was a night watchman at a factory, they started begging him to let them

A Chassidic family makes a clandestine living

sleep over.

Otherwise, they told him, they would have to walk the freezing streets all night with no place to lay their heads.

Father could not refuse. He told one Jew to knock at the door a set number of times at an agreed time to be let in. Soon word got around and another begged him and another. Before long, a large group of Jews came regularly every night to sleep over in the warm building, leaving before the first workers arrived.

One Jew brought in a cooker to make supper for everyone, boiling eggs or potatoes. Others brought Torah books, and soon the factory turned into a nightly Beis HaMedrash!

Father was exposing himself to grave risk. Aside from

abusing his employer's confidence, he could be accused of running clandestine religious activities. But his conscience would have given him no rest if he hadn't helped them. He was overjoyed at the chance to help fellow Jews in need of a warm place for the night.

Perhaps neighbors noticed something unusual. Maybe the manager himself got suspicious. One night he suddenly walked in and discovered the whole group. He threw them all out, seizing their Torah books in order to show them to the secret police to check for possible counter-revolutionary material. Of course, Father was fired on the spot.

Whenever anyone was dismissed from work, his employer had to complete a form specifying how long he had worked, when he was dismissed, and the reason why. Understandably, the manager was hopping mad about the incident and wanted to write that Father was utterly irresponsible and unreliable.

"How can you write such a thing about a fellow Jew?" Father begged him tearfully. "If the form is filled out like that, I'll never get a job anywhere! Have pity, I have a wife and children!"

The manager's Jewish heart was stirred. He wrote simply that Father was dismissed due to "unsuitability to the needs of the plant," thus enabling him to find another job.

TWO WEDDINGS

The needs of others always came first, before Father's and those of his family. Here is another example, a few years later:

At that time, Yeshiva students were on the run. Three of them, Nechemia Liss, Zalman Leib Estulin and a third student, were in hiding in the attic of the renowned Lubavitcher Shul in the Marina Roshcha district of Moscow, where they studied Torah day and night.

Their material needs were supplied by kind Jews including Father.

In Moscow lived Reb Zalman Sudakevitch (now in Kfar Chabad), a very successful businessman. Once Father approached him for help, telling him that a fine match had been found for Nechemia Liss.

Although it was hard to find apartments for newlyweds, Reb Yisroel Kok was building a house in a Moscow suburb and was looking for buyers, preferably Torah-observant Jews. Each one-room apartment cost 10,000 rubles. If that money could be raised, the couple could marry and establish a new Jewish family.

Reb Zalman generously pledged half the sum - 5,000 rubles.

Father was overjoyed, telling him he would raise the rest from other kind Jews.

Then Father added, bashfully: "Actually, I'm interested in having Zalman Leib Estulin as a husband for my own daughter. Of course, I would need an apartment for them, too. But I'm not sure that I am permitted by the Torah to raise funds for them when I'm raising funds for Nechemia..."

Reb Zalman - amazed at how Father was concerned first for someone unrelated to him while he himself needed help

Reb Zalman Leib Estulin, my brother-in-law, with his wife, my sister Reizel, and some of their family

for his own daughter - immediately doubled his pledge and added 5,000 rubles for my sister's wedding expenses!

To solve Father's "problem," Reb Zalman suggested he tell donors he was raising funds to help two couples get married, one of whom was Nechemia Liss and his fiancée. Father did that, and before long both weddings were celebrated, one a week after the other!

NEW SHOES FOR A YESHIVA STUDENT

Whoever knew Father agrees that his most outstanding quality was his kindness of heart. To enumerate all of his many good deeds would be impossible. We will suffice with but one more:

Rabbi Lippe Schapiro (now Rabbi of the Empire Shtiebel

synagogue in Crown Heights) was a student at the Lubavitcher Yeshiva in Kharkov. Once, when Father was staying there, he was talking with Lippe and in the course of conversation, happened to ask him his shoe-size. Without thinking anything unusual about the question, Lippe told him his size. How amazed Lippe was the next day when Father presented him with a brand new pair of shoes! He had noticed that Lippe's old ones were ripped and did not want a Yeshiva student to have torn shoes.

That was at a time when Father had no bread to put into his own mouth...

CORRESPONDENCE WITH THE LUBAVITCHER REBBE

Although Father was not a Lubavitcher, he was very close with the Lubavitcher Chassidim, admiring their self-sacrifice for preserving Yiddishkeit. In recent years I discovered that Father once wrote to the Previous Lubavitcher Rebbe, Rabbi Yosef Yitzchok Schneersohn (1880-1950), and received a reply from him. Amazingly, Father's letter and a copy of the Rebbe's reply are preserved to this day in the archives of the central Lubavitch Library in Crown Heights, Brooklyn. Here is a translation of Father's letter:

"By the grace of G-d, third day of the week of the Torah portion 'And may they be for a remembrance before G-d,' in the year of 'Yeshua V'rachamim' [deliverance and mercy – 5695-1935].

"To his honored Holiness, the Rebbe, long may he live:

The Lubavitcher Rebbe, Rabbi Yosef Yitzchok Schneersohn, in Brooklyn, New York

"I, the young man Chayim Binyomin, while not acquainted with you, am compelled to let you know some of my deeds and concerns performed for your young men studying at Kharkov in order that they not be disturbed from their study of the holy Torah. Thank G-d, I have supplied them with all their material needs, doing kindness for them physically, spiritually and financially, thank G-d. While I was with your acquaintances,members of your [Chabad Chassidic] community, Reb YitzchokMasmid with whom I traveled to Mezibuzh to be at the holy grave site of the Baal Shem Tov, of blessed memory, and Reb Yehoshua Volosov etc., and in general with all of them, there was great affection between us, thank G-d.

"Now, in recent years, too, I happen to be with members of your [Chabad Chassidic] community in the city of Moscow.

"Folle Boruch Sholom's [Reb Refoel Kahan, son of Reb Boruch Sholom] is acquainted with me, and knows me and everything that has happened to me, may the Merciful One save us. Thank G-d, now he is a free man [he was allowed to leave the USSR].

"I, on the other hand, am forced to work for low wages that are not enough even for a little bread, and I have the responsibility of supporting and raising my family members to Torah study and fear of G-d.

"Therefore I ask, please, in the goodness of your heart, please bestow Tzedaka [charity] on me and send me assistance.

"For the [anti-religious] peril here for young people is

well-known, and I don't have enough to pay for tuition, clothing and shoes. From where can I supply them? My heart is broken within me for fear that perhaps he [my son] may leave me, G-d forbid, and go, G-d forbid, in their [non-religious] ways as a result of my poverty, may the Merciful One save us. If only I could supply him with shoes and all his needs. He is a truly fine religious boy, and he respects me, thank G-d. But because he suffers embarrassment [as a result of the poverty], I am an embarrassment to him.

"May G-d have mercy upon you. May there be fulfilled in you the verses 'He sows charities, He causes deliverance to sprout forth,' 'and the deed of charity shall be peace.' I beg of you, and hope you will not turn me away empty-handed.

"From me, Chayim Binyomin Brod.

"I send regards to all my acquaintances who are with you."

The Rebbe's replies to the USSR were not mailed directly in order to avoid endangering the recipients (for the "crime" of corresponding with foreigners, especially with the Rebbe, whom they considered "the Soviet Union's number-one enemy"). Instead, a number of replies would be sent - perhaps by someone traveling to the USSR - to a follower of the Rebbe there who would then forward them to their destinations.

The Rebbe sent his reply to Father in the month of Kislev, 5696 (end of 1935). Here is a translation of the copy preserved in the archives (Igros Kodesh of the Rebbe RaYYaTz, XI, p. 275):

My father's letter to the Rebbe,
preserved to this day in the central Lubavitcher archives

"Brod, Uman:

"...Concerning help for you with any financial assistance. G-d willing, at the first opportunity I shall try for you. May G-d provide you with your livelihood so that you may raise your children to Torah study, marriage and good deeds, in conditions of ample livelihood, without stress. Please give my regards to those who participate in the Torah study groups, and inform them of my blessing that G-d help them materially and spiritually."

The Rebbe kept his word and did send Father a one-time stipend, as Father later told me.

"BUT I'M ABLE TO VISIT MY REBBE!"

Father was deeply sensitive. Everything affected him to the very core of his heart. Here is one memorable example:

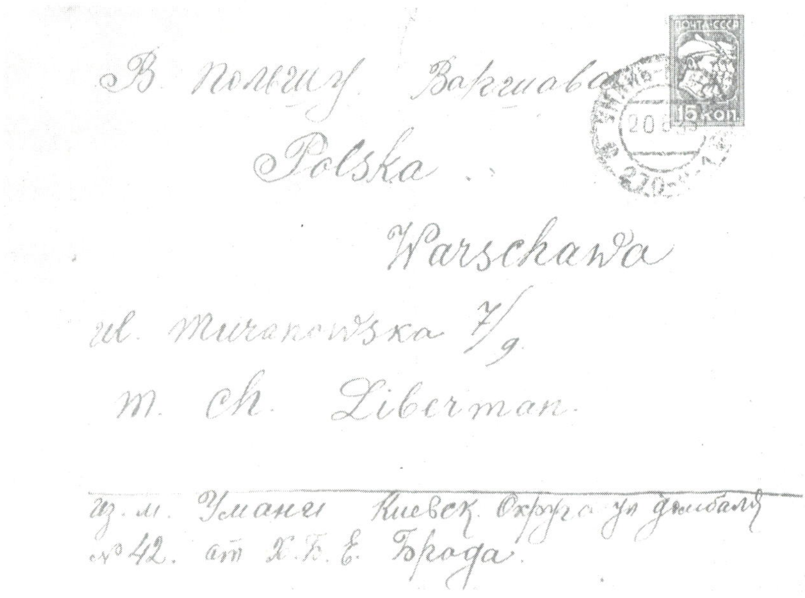

The envelope in which my father sent his letter to the Rebbe

At the end of 1933, I spent some time with Father in Moscow.

A Chassidic holiday came up - I think it was Yud-Tes Kislev, the anniversary of the passing in 1772 of Rabbi DovBer, Maggid of Mezeritch, the Baal Shem Tov's successor as leader of Chassidism, and also of the 1798 release from Czarist imprisonment of his great disciple Rabbi Shneur Zalman (1745-1812), the Alter Rebbe, founder of the Chabad-Lubavitch school of Chassidism.

Since it was a Chassidic holiday, Father wanted to participate in a "Farbrengen" - a gathering of Chassidim to celebrate. We traveled to Malachovka, an outer suburb of Moscow, where a community of Lubavitchers lived, led by the well-known Chossid Rabbi Yaakov Meskalik - known as "Yankel Zhuravitzer" (by the name of his town rather than his family name, as was customary in Lubavitch and elsewhere years ago).

During the Farbrengen, Reb Yankel started to sing the Chassidic song of yearning for one's Rebbe (to the tune of "Kol Dodi" by the Alter Rebbe): "Der Eibershter zol geben gezunt un leben, vellen mir zich zehen mit unzer Rebben!" - "May G-d grant us good health and life so that we may meet with our Rebbe!" Reb Yankel sang it from the very depths of his heart, with every fiber of his soul, weeping bitterly at the enforced distance from his Rebbe, Rabbi Yosef Yitzchok, who had left for Riga, Latvia, in 1927.

After the Farbrengen, we traveled back to our room in Moscow.

Soon I noticed Father packing. "Are you leaving,

Rabbi Yaakov Meskalik ("Zhuravitzer")

Father?"

"Yes," he replied, "I'm going back to Uman!"

"Why suddenly now?" I asked.

"Didn't we just see Reb Yankel crying bitterly how he yearns to see his Rebbe?" asked Father. "Unfortunately, he can't visit his Rebbe. But I'm able to go visit mine!"

And off we left on the 500-kilometer trip to Uman, to the grave of Father's Rebbe, Rabbi Nachman of Breslov!

DANCING IN JAIL

Father was arrested on several occasions, though he was never detained for a very long time, thank G-d. In Moscow, he was once arrested on a Friday and thrown into jail. Immediately his friends sent a telegram to our family in Uman, conveying the news in disguised language to conceal its meaning from the secret police:

"Father is sick and has been taken to the hospital."

After a brief investigation, the police realized he was not the one they sought. On Shabbos morning the jailer brought Father a release form to sign.

"Sorry," Father told him, "on the Sabbath I don't write!"

"What?" the jailer yelled angrily. "You're a religious fanatic, too?"

But it made no difference. Father refused to sign on Shabbos.

The jailer had never encountered anyone actually refusing to be released from jail! Assuming Father would soon change his mind, he threw him back into his cell.

But the jailer's amazement grew as Father burst into song and started dancing! Later Father explained that until then he had considered his imprisonment a punishment for his sins. But now his continued stay in jail was only for observing G-d's commandment of keeping Shabbos – a thought so inspiring that he danced in joy...

The jailer tried again to get him to leave. But Father played the fool: "Why should I want to leave? Here I have a place to lie down, and bread to satisfy my hunger. I want to stay!"

Seeing that Father was not his normal jailbird, the jailer asked him: "So when would you agree to leave?"

"At night, when three stars appear in the sky. Then I'll go out fast so that I can dance with the moon..."

After nightfall, the jailer came to tell him that three stars had appeared. Father signed his release form and left.

Back at his friends' home, his release was cause for great celebration. To be released so fast was a miracle, as was the fact that he had not been punished for refusing to leave when he was ordered to. Father was convinced that someone in our family in Uman must have gone to the grave of his Rebbe, Rabbi Nachman, to pray for him. Indeed my sister Tzivia had spent all day there, pouring out her heart in prayer for Father's release.

DAY OF JUDGMENT

Another time that Father was arrested was in 1941. When Germany attacked the USSR in World War II, my parents, like thousands of other Jews, fled to Central Asia (I was then in Yeshiva in Gruzia – Soviet Georgia). Settling in Tashkent, Father made a living selling medications on the black market.

Many Jewish refugees from Poland had escaped there, too, and one of them started doing business with Father. My sister Tzivia thought him suspicious and told Father so. But she had nothing tangible on which to base her suspicions, so Father saw no reason to give up the profitable deals the man brought him.

Sure enough, the man showed up one day with a policeman, who arrested Father. For many months he suffered terribly in jail.

Besides his brutal treatment by jailers and interrogators, other prisoners made his life a misery, robbing him of everything he received from home, including clothes and even his shoes.

His trial was set for Rosh Hashana.

That Rosh Hashana morning, the Lubavitcher Chassidim were praying at the home of the Chossid Reb Yechiel Yosef Rivkin.

Suddenly my younger brother Yisroel, aged six, stepped

before the Aron Kodesh (holy ark containing the Sefer Torah scroll) and burst into tears.

"Jews!" he wept in a heart-rending voice. "Today is G-d's Day of Judgment for the whole world. And it's also the day of my father's judgment by the Communists. I beg you: Pray to G-d that He save my father, otherwise I and my sisters may fall into their wicked hands!" Hearing the little boy pleading for his father's life was so moving that everyone present burst into tears. Mother even fainted from the pent-up emotion that her little son had now brought to a head.

My sister Tzivia waited outside to watch out for Father as they brought him to court. From far off she noticed two men approaching, who appeared to be non-Jews. One was tall and upright, the other short and bent over, his head lowered.

Suddenly, the truth struck her like a dagger to her heart. No, it couldn't be! The bent-over man was Father! His jailers had shaved off his beard and were dragging him barefoot with his head uncovered. Stung with shame, Father kept his eyes on the ground. No one could have imagined that such a happy soul always brimming with joy could be reduced to such a pitiable state...

Thank G-d, the Jews' impassioned prayers that Rosh Hashana had their effect on High. The judge decided that the time Father had spent in jail was punishment enough and ordered him released.

At their makeshift Shul, the Jews were preparing to blow the Shofar. The prominent Chassidim, including the renowned Chossid Rabbi Yisroel Levin (known as "Yisroel Neveler"), were gathered around the Torah-reading table.

Just then the good news arrived. Reb Yisroel looked up, his Talis (prayer-shawl) falling from his head to his shoulders, and declared with heartfelt emotion: "Thank You, G-d! Thank You, G-d!"

HOW PRECIOUS A DAY OF TORAH STUDY!

Mother was born in Mezibuzh. She was always a true companion to Father, lovingly accepting any suffering resulting from Father's life of sacrifice. Never did she complain about our poverty, even when Father devoted himself to other's needs at the expense of his own family's necessities.

Seeing how Mother suffered and often went without food for our sake, we felt her sacrifice and lovingly accepted our hunger and poverty without complaint.

After the 1917 Bolshevik Revolution, the regime closed all Yeshivos and Chadorim (Torah schools). However, Torah-observant parents established secret Chadorim for their children.

We left for Cheder at the same time other children left for school so as not to arouse suspicion. Before I left, Mother gave me a little food to eat and sent a little extra for lunchtime, as coming home during the day would have attracted attention.

One morning, when I was about six or seven, Mother woke me as usual. She told me she had a request to ask of me. But first, she said, I must promise to do as she asked. Of course, I agreed.

"Chatzkele," she told me, "I have no food in the house to give you. Even so, I'm asking you to go to Cheder as usual. Soon, I hope, I'll be able to borrow a few pennies and buy some bread, which I'll bring you at Cheder."

The night before I had gone without supper. It was a time of famine throughout Russia. People were starving for bread. We had almost become accustomed to not eating. Sometimes we saved a meal by doing without supper, on other days by missing our daytime meal.

I was famished. But I understood the situation and agreed to go.

At Cheder we said the morning prayers and started our Torah studies. I tried not to think about my growling hunger pangs. But as the hours passed, I felt my strength ebbing. I walked over to my teacher and told him I did not feel well. The hunger must have been apparent on my face, for he immediately suggested I go home.

We lived on a small hill. I remember bounding up the hill on the way home to get there faster. Then I remember no more.

When I came to, I was lying on the ground soaked in water.

Apparently, the neighbors had rushed over with buckets of water to revive me when I fainted.

Later, a close friend and neighbor of Mother berated her: "Why did you send Chatzkele to Cheder that day? You knew he hadn't eaten for so long and must be feeling weak. Why didn't you wait till you had some bread to give him and then send him to Cheder, or even keep him home for the

My mother, with my younger brother Yisroel, aged about one year old

day?"

"No!" replied Mother. "At a time like this, every day of Torah study is more precious than gold. I wouldn't want to bear the responsibility for a Jewish child losing even one day of Torah study at Cheder!"

MOTHER'S SIMPLE FAITH

Mother was full of faith. She brought us up, too, to have faith in G-d and His servants – the Tzaddikim (saintly personalities) – together with deep Yiras Shomayim (awe of G-d).

Years later, after I came to the United States, I was surprised when the Chossid Reb Yochanon Gordon (who passed away in 1969), Gabbai of the Rebbe's Shul at 770

Eastern Parkway, Crown Heights, once asked me how my mother was. I found his question surprising. He could not have known my parents, for he had never lived in the Soviet Union; his hometown Dokshitz was in Lithuania, from where he had emigrated to the United States before World War II. Nor were we so close that he should ask me about my family members.

Noticing my surprise, he explained why he was asking. He had met a Jew from Russia named Reb Mendel Maizes, who had settled in New York. Mendel had a brother, Reb Avrohom Eliyohu Maizes, who was unusually devout: During Elul (the last month before the High Holidays), for example, he would spend the whole month in service of G-d to ensure that his repentance be sincere. Although not a Chossid, he had heard of the deeply religious atmosphere of Uman and repeatedly suggested to Mendel – who at that time needed reinforcement in his Jewish observance and faith in G-d – to spend a Shabbos there. Eventually Mendel agreed.

Arriving in Uman, he had gone to Shul. But he felt uncomfortable there, not knowing anyone. Fortunately, Father greeted him with a hearty "Sholom Aleichem!" and asked him all about himself. He then invited him to eat with the family for Shabbos.

It was a short winter Friday. During the day Reb Mendel came in to talk with Father and was shocked by what he saw. Our home was freezing, and we children lay huddled under threadbare blankets.

Mother told him simply that Father had gone to Rabbi

Nachman's grave "to ask the Rebbe for our needs for Shabbos..."

Mother made this statement so naturally, with such simple faith, that Mendel's heart was touched.

Seeing the family's grinding poverty, he reminded himself of the fifteen rubles he had kept for his train fare home. He found himself saying: "Oh, I forgot, Reb Chayim Binyomin asked me to give you this to prepare for Shabbos." And he handed over the fifteen rubles – all the money he had...

Mother was a fast worker. In no time at all, she had a fire burning in the stove, had bought food, prepared and cooked it. By the time Father came home the whole Shabbos was ready!

It was a happy and satisfying Shabbos, with ample food on the table. Mendel spent long hours with Father in joyous song and lively discussion. That Shabbos left a deep impression on him.

After Shabbos, Mendel had to get back home. But he had no money for the fare. Then he reminded himself that he had bought a lottery ticket that week. When he checked his luck, he discovered that, with G-d's help, he had won twenty-five rubles – more than enough for his fare home!

Years later, he told Reb Yochanon Gordon that that Shabbos had left an indelible mark on him. Most of all he had been inspired by Mother's simple statement that Father had gone to Rabbi Nachman's grave to ask for their Shabbos needs. She had said it so naturally, as a wife today might mention how her husband has gone to the bank to cash a check! Her simple, heartfelt faith had moved him beyond words...

Reb Yochanan told me he had even repeated this story to the Rebbe, who had enjoyed hearing it.

"Now do you understand why I'm asking how your mother is?"

DIVINE PROVIDENCE

My parents lived on miracles, barely eking out a living week by week. Sometimes they managed to earn a little money, sometimes they borrowed, and sometimes, as in the previous story, our salvation came from an utterly unexpected source.

One Friday morning there was nothing in the house for Shabbos.

Father went out to look for someone who could give him a loan. As he walked through the streets, he heard someone calling his name.

It was a fellow Breslover Chossid named Moshe Shmuel.

"Chayim Binyomin, I'm so glad to meet you! This morning I came back from Kiev, and I've got something for you. A Jew named Pinchas Sudak, when he heard that I was returning to Uman, sent with me ten rubles to give you for Shadchonus!"

Father was utterly taken aback. "Shadchonus" means commission for arranging a match between a couple that gets married. But Father had no recollection of anyone called Pinchas Sudak, or of having arranged any match for him. But Moshe Shmuel insisted that he was just a messenger and had no further information.

Although he was puzzled, Father saw the clear hand of Divine Providence in that the money had arrived just then, for in the course of nature there seemed no other way to be able to make Shabbos that week. Asking no more questions, he took the money.

It was some time before he learned why he had received the Shadchonus money.

Father traveled through many towns in Russia. While in Ruzhin, the local Shochet had asked him whether he had encountered on his travels any fine, Torah-observant young men suitable for his three eligible daughters. Father promised to look out for him.

Later, Father passed through the town where Pinchas Sudak's parents lived. They asked if he knew of a religious girl for their son Pinchas. Father immediately gave them the Shochet's address in Ruzhin and thought no more of it.

The Sudaks contacted the Shochet, arranged for their son to meet one of his daughters, and the match was made. The newly married couple settled in Kiev and several years passed. They already had children by the time Pinchas heard one day that Moshe Shmuel was leaving for Uman, where Chayim Binyomin Brod lived, and recalled his long-overdue debt for Father's Shadchonus!

The Shochet's other two daughters married Lubavitchers: Reb Hirshel Malchik, and Rabbi Yisroel Leibov, who later lived in Kfar Chabad and was the first and long-time director of the Lubavitch Youth Organization of Israel.

Reb Pinchas Sudak's son, Nachman, learned for many

years in Yeshivas Tomchei Tmimim and now heads the Lubavitch movement in England. His two sisters also are married to Lubavitchers.

STAYING IN THE HOLY LAND

For many years, my parents tried to leave the Soviet Union. Year by year they would apply for exit permits, only to be refused, which meant waiting another year of heartache before reapplying. After years of frustration, they were finally granted their permits to leave in 5722 (1962). In those days, receiving such a permit was unprecedented, and it sparked boundless joy both for them and their family members and also for other Torah-observant Jews in the USSR who now saw a faint ray of hope shining through at the end of their long dark night...

At the Bar Mitzva of my nephew, Dovid Astulin, after my brother Yisroel and his family arrived in the Holy Land

They emigrated to Israel, settling in Bnei Brak. When Father arrived at Lod airport, he was so excited at being privileged to reach the Holy Land that he bent down to kiss its sacred soil! He started dancing so exuberantly that scores of people gathered around to watch the unusual sight.

When Torah-observant Jews in the Soviet Union heard about Father's joyous dancing in public at the airport, they feared it might be interpreted as a dance of victory over the Soviets and as an excuse to refuse exit permits to other Jews.

Years later someone who had been in the Soviet secret police revealed that they had indeed been aware of Father's exuberance at the airport but had attributed no special significance to it, as he used to dance like that while still in the Soviet Union...

(Contrary to what many in the free world assume, it is clear from here and other known incidents how the Soviets had an uncanny knowledge of everything going on in other countries. Their spy net embraced Israel and the United States among other lands, and there were sufficient grounds for those who had left the Soviet Union to conceal information that could jeopardize those left behind.)

After my parents reached the Holy Land, I often invited them to come to the United States to visit my family. Although they would have loved to see my family and also to meet the Rebbe, Father always replied that now that they had been privileged to reach the Holy Land, he was reluctant to leave.

Father passed away on Shabbos, 21 Kislev, 5731 (1970).

After immersing himself in the Mikvah before Shabbos, he went to Shul for the afternoon prayers, then returned home saying that he did not feel well. He lay down and passed away a short while later.

Mother passed away on 9 Adar I, 5738 (1978). Both are buried at the cemetery of Har Hamenuchot, Jerusalem.

My parents had five children. The eldest was my late sister Reizel, who married Reb Zalman Leib Estulin. They left the Soviet Union for Israel in 1966. I was born next, and then came my sister Tzivia, who left the Soviet Union in 1946 at the same time as I, and married Reb Yaakov Galinsky, settling eventually in Bnei Brak. Next was my sister Soroh, who married Reb Yaakov Lepkivker. In 1969, they left the Soviet Union with their family and also settled in Bnei Brak. The youngest was my brother Yisroel, married to Perel'a, who left the Soviet Union with his family in 1965 and settled in Kfar Chabad.

CHAPTER THREE

A CHILD IN EXILE

I BECOME THREE YEARS YOUNGER

Soviet regulations required all residents to be registered at their place of abode, supplying the municipal offices with personal data about all family members – their date and place of birth, where they had come from, and the exact date they had arrived at the location. The government had no way of checking all this information for accuracy, but it recorded the information on the personal identification documents it issued.

When we moved from Mezibuzh to Uman in 1931, my sister Reizel was eleven. But Father registered her as several years older so that she would be above school age. I was eight, the age for starting school. As I was small for my age, Father registered me as five, thereby putting off the problem for a few years.

"As long as I live," Father often declared, "no child of mine will attend any Soviet government school." The

Jewish schools were the worst, run by Jewish Communists who worked hard to implant atheism in their pupils' minds and turn them into ardent Communists. I once heard that the Breslover Chassidic elders had ruled that if anyone's children would be forced to attend a government school, it was better to enroll them at a non-Jewish school than at a Jewish Communist one.

Meanwhile I studied at the local underground Cheder until I was ten and a half. Expecting problems later that year with the school authorities, my parents decided to send me away. If the Uman school authorities asked about me, they could truthfully reply that I was out of town. On the other hand, the authorities in the other city would not be aware of my presence at all.

A STRANGER IN KHARKOV

Friends of the family recommended sending me to Kharkov, where the underground Chadorim were not then actively persecuted by the authorities. So began the long wanderings of my youth. Father accompanied me on the long 500 kilometer train ride to Kharkov. He himself was leaving for Moscow - 650 kilometers distance from Kharkov - where he hoped to make a living.

He left me in the care of several kind Jews and said goodbye.

At ten years old I was left alone, many hundreds of miles from my parents and sister.

I was a very shy child. My greatest embarrassment was to eat at the home of strangers, especially if other children

Proletarian Square in Kharkov

were there.

The first Friday evening I was invited by a fine respectable Jew (whose name I have forgotten) to stay for Shabbos with his family. When we came home from Shul, his young children pierced me with their childish stares, and I was overcome with embarrassment.

All through the meal I kept my eyes on my plate, barely tasting the food. My only thought was how soon the meal would be over so that I could escape. Afterwards they gave me a bed for the night, and the next morning I accompanied my host to Shul.

I couldn't bear enduring that experience again and I resolved not to go back for the Shabbos morning meal. After prayers, I hid between two big benches so that the man would not find me. Being so small and thin, I managed to escape his notice. He looked all over for me, but eventually gave up and went home. I stayed at Shul, preferring not to eat all day rather than to suffer the embarrassment of eating at a strange home. After Mincha prayers, towards evening, when a Shalosh Seudos meal was served at Shul, I took a piece of bread from the table, crept off to a quiet corner, and stilled my hunger.

After Shabbos I found a way of letting Father know that I refused to stay any longer in Kharkov. As soon as a reliable Jew was found who was traveling to Moscow, I accompanied him there, later proceeding back with Father to Uman (a round trip of over 1,000 kilometers).

ESCAPE FROM THE PRINCIPAL

My parents realized that I was still too young to be away from home. Back I went to study at the Cheder in Uman.

Months passed and I turned eleven, or eight according to the town registry. Letters started arriving from the school authorities telling my parents to enroll me at school for the coming year.

Mother just ignored them while Father was then in Moscow.

One day, at the end of Tammuz (July), I noticed through the window that the principal of the Jewish government school was walking in our direction. To my horror, he turned towards our door.

There was no doubt in my mind that because my parents had neglected to enroll me at his school for the coming year, he had come to do it himself...

I jumped out of a window and hid. Only Mother was home. She opened the door and they sat down to talk. I have no idea what he said or what Mother answered, but after a short while he left.

The danger was past and I went back inside. But it was clear now to me, too, that I could stay no longer in Uman.

Recently we had heard of a Torah-study program in Kiev at my level, with material conditions that were suitable. It was also much closer to Uman, just 200 kilometers away. So it was decided that I leave for Kiev without delay.

KIEV

Kiev is a most impressive city. The old part of the city is one of the most beautiful in Russia. But for me it arouses above all fond memories of its wonderful Jewish

Kiev, looking out towards the Dnieper River that bisects the city

atmosphere.

Most of all I was impressed by Rabbi Aryeh Leib Kaplan, to whose home I was directed to go in Kiev. Despite his poverty he greeted me warmly and immediately made me feel at home, accepting me as part of the family.

At that time, he and his wife had just one little girl at home. Their older daughter was already married to Rabbi Yitzchok Mekubetsky, while their sons – Rabbi Elimelech (later Rosh Yeshiva of Yeshivas Tomchei Tmimim in Lod, Israel) and Rabbi Moshe Binyomin (who later lived many years in Crown Heights and is now in Jerusalem) – were on the move, studying at underground Lubavitcher Yeshivos in various cities.

Rabbi Aryeh Leib Kaplan, whose wonderful personality is deeply engraved in my heart

Rabbi Kaplan studied Torah all day at the Kupetcheske ("Merchants") Shul, where many other Jews also spent their days in prayer and study – a rare phenomenon by then. Great sums were raised for charity there, far more than the congregants could afford. Many daily study-groups were taught by Torah scholars, on "Ein Yaakov" and other subjects. Rabbi Kaplan taught a daily lesson on "Chok L'Yisroel," for which he was paid 100 rubles a month. That was his only income, barely enough to support his family.

Besides giving me meals and a place to stay, Rabbi Kaplan taught me Torah for some time every day. Afterwards I would go to the Slomonki district where Velvel Averbach (now in Crown Heights) lived, and I would study with him. One home where we learned was that of Reb Yitzchok Zakon, at 5 Oritsky Street. Together with several other boys, including Reb Yitzchok's son Aharon (now in Crown Heights), we studied under Reb Shaul Eliyahu Orul, who taught us TaNaCh (Scripture), Kitzur Shulchan Aruch and similar studies.

For me it was a well-organized Torah study program with very satisfactory living conditions.

On Shabbos, I would go to Shul accompanied by Rebbetzin Kaplan – Rabbi Kaplan apparently attended a

Kiev's central square

Shul in a different part of the city. Once neighbors asked her about the little boy who accompanied her, always so deep in thought. She told them that I was not well and perhaps I was worried about my sickness. Actually, whenever I was in the street, my constant worry was how to avoid getting a rock thrown at my head, for several times non-Jewish kids had grabbed me and beaten me up...

NOT SO EASY

After spending two summer months in Kiev, I went back home for the Jewish holidays of the month of Tishrei. We were happy to be together again, but I had to stay hidden so that neighbors would not inform the school principal that I was back in town.

After Simchas Torah, I returned to Kiev. But when I arrived at Rabbi Kaplan's home, he took me aside and, obviously very pained at having to tell me this, explained that his economic situation had taken a turn for the worse. I was welcome to continue sleeping there, but unfortunately he could no longer give me meals.

There was no choice but to revert to the old Yeshiva student system of "essen teg," eating meals each day at different families who volunteered in this way to help students learn Torah.

But I was still shy, especially at homes where children were present. When I was too embarrassed to go to someone's home, as often happened, I preferred going hungry all day. If I had a few pennies in my pocket I bought some bread to still my hunger.

Kiev's city center

Otherwise I starved. For me, embarrassment was worse than hunger.

SPECIAL JEWS

Kiev had several Jewish districts permeated with a wonderful atmosphere of Torah, Chassidus and Yiras Shomayim. Many Torah-observant Jews lived in Naiyovke, while others lived in Podol. One resident in Podol was Reb Henoch Rapaport, with whom I had many long conversations.

The Slomonki district had a fine Jewish community, with many outstanding personalities. Reb Moshe Kolikov, a Hornestaipler Chossid, had a beard and Peyos – both increasingly rare in those days. He had become wealthy from dealing in depreciated merchandise. Every Shabbos, at Shalosh Seudos, he would deliver a Chassidic Torah teaching with such deep emotion, literally in tears, that everyone was moved.

Other wonderful Jews I remember from that district include Reb Pinye Katcher, Reb Moshe Vinarsker, Rabbi Eliyahu and Rabbi Naftoli (I don't know their last names). It is difficult to describe all these extraordinary personalities adequately. One Shabbos I was invited to eat at Rabbi Naftoli's home and afterwards he invited me to join him in study of the "Or Hachayim" commentary (by Rabbi Chayim Ibn Attar, 1696-1743) on that week's Torah portion of "B'shalach." He explained it so well that I remember it till today.

MESIRAS NEFESH FOR A MIKVAH

One outstanding personality in Kiev who left a deep impression on me was Reb Isaac Lipshitz, then about eighty years old. Before the Revolution he had been very wealthy, but the Communists had confiscated his wealth. Somehow he had managed to save some of it and, having no children of his own, used it for helping other Jews.

Reb Isaac had a free loan fund, used especially by Jews who refused to work on Shabbos. Many such Jews made a living from home industries and secret businesses, for which they often needed advance cash for buying merchandise. They could always get a loan from Reb Isaac, cheerfully and in a way that preserved their self-respect.

He also operated a network of secret Cheder schools, paying the salaries of perhaps twenty teachers. Reb Isaac would gather together boys who wanted to learn Torah but whose parents could not afford tuition, organizing them in small classes at private homes.

It took incredible courage for Reb Isaac to maintain a Mikvah in the city. Before the Revolution, every Jewish community had its own Mikvah for women to observe their monthly immersion in keeping with the important Torah obligation of Taharas Hamishpacha (Jewish marital purity). But the Communists had forcibly closed all Mikvaos except in a few large cities such as Moscow, Leningrad and Kharkov where they preserved them as showcases to the world to prove the Soviet "freedom of religion."

Kiev, however, had no legal Mikvah. So Reb Isaac, at great personal risk, decided to build a secret one. He bought a private house and built a Mikvah there that lasted for several months.

Apparently neighbors noticed "suspicious" movements every evening and informed the police, who closed it down. Reb Isaac bought a second house and built another Mikvah. But neighbors reported that one too, and the police closed it.

There had to be a better way. Then an idea struck him. In Kiev there was a factory producing tracks for tanks, which operated in three shifts around the clock. Reb Isaac bought a broken-down house near the factory and converted it into a Mikvah. The constant movement to and from the factory at all hours of the day ensured that women coming to use the Mikvah never aroused any suspicion!

No one knew of this Mikvah except those who had to know, for anyone involved could have gotten into serious trouble. Reb Isaac himself would stoke the furnace every day, while his wife devotedly took care of everything else.

How did I find out about it? Reb Isaac was a friend of Rabbi Kaplan and, on one winter Thursday afternoon, he invited him to immerse himself before the women arrived in the evening. Rabbi Kaplan took me with him. Never would I have believed that a Mikvah could be located in such an unlikely place!

Jews like Reb Isaac had true Mesiras Nefesh to preserve Torah and Mitzvos, which left an unforgetable impression upon me.

THE SHUL IS CLOSED

A painful memory for me was the day in 5696 (1936) when the Kupetcheske Shul was taken over by the government. As happened in Jewish communities all over Russia, the government decided to requisition the Shul, giving the congregants a date by which to vacate it and remove its holy books.

The Jewish community was thunderstruck. A three-day fast was proclaimed, with Tehilim (Psalms) recited in shifts around the clock. Again and again the entire community read Psalm 83, verse by verse: "G-d, do not hold Yourself silent, be not deaf and be not quiet, O G-d. For here Your enemies are in uproar and those who hate You have raised their head... They have said, 'Come, let us destroy them from being a nation, so that the name of Israel be remembered no longer!' "

Tragically, the prayers were of no avail. On the set date, Jews filled the Shul from end to end, each wearing his Talis (prayer shawl) and Tefilin. But soldiers mounted on horses surrounded the Shul while others armed with clubs broke in, beating the Jews inside brutally until they forced them out.

Then the soldiers started throwing the Sefer Torah scrolls and holy books outside in a huge pile in front of the Shul. There was no choice but to take them to another Shul, a small one at 8 Supasky Street, a holy task in which I participated. It was a tragic day of shame for Kiev Jewry.

GOODBYE TO KIEV

Moshe Binyomin Kaplan

In Kiev I spent close to three years. Rabbi Kaplan's son Moshe Binyomin was studying then at a branch of the Lubavitcher Yeshiva in Zhitomir – together with, among others, the late Rabbi Moshe Aharon Geisinsky, who later lived in Crown Heights for many years.

Before Pesach, 1937, Moshe Binyomin wrote home that a Yeshiva for boys of my age was opening in Berditchev – about 180 kilometers from Uman – and recommended that I go there after returning home for Pesach.

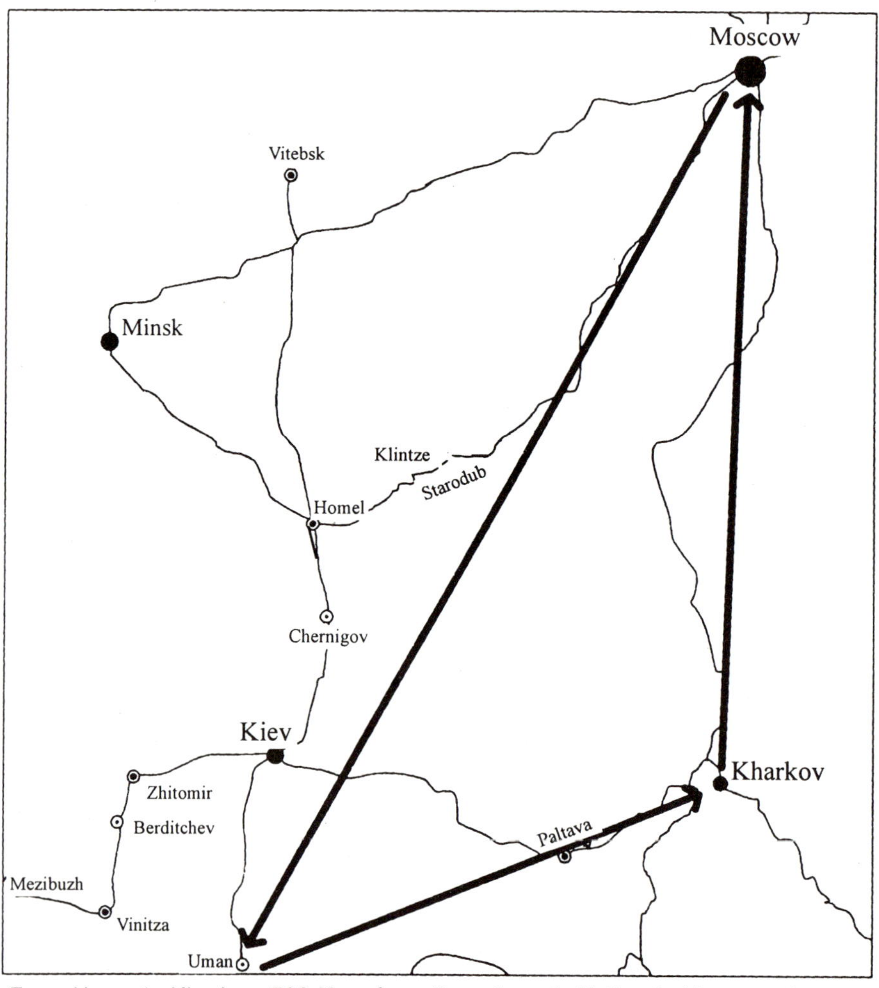

From Uman to Kharkov, 500 Km., from there I ran to Father in Moscow, then back home to Uman

CHAPTER FOUR

YESHIVAS TOMCHEI TMIMIM

I BECOME A YESHIVA BOCHUR

At that time, several Jewish communities still had underground Chadorim for younger students. But for older students only one Yeshiva remained in the Soviet Union: the Lubavitcher Yeshiva.

Known as "Tomchei Tmimim," this Yeshiva had originally been established in 1897 in the town of Lubavitch by the fifth leader of Chabad, the Rebbe RaShaB, Rabbi Sholom DovBer Schneersohn (1860-1920), father of Rabbi Yosef Yitzchok, whom he appointed the Yeshiva's dean as soon as it was founded. After the 1917 Revolution, the Yeshiva was forced to wander from one town to another to avoid being disbanded by the regime, later splitting into smaller groups that could more easily escape detection.

This Yeshiva's unique Chassidic atmosphere was legendary. I had heard so much about it that I hoped and prayed to be privileged one day to be among its students.

Reb Moshe Rubinson, our Rosh Yeshiva, teaching students

Now that great day had arrived.

BERDITCHEV

A new branch of the Yeshiva for young teenaged students was opening after Pesach in Berditchev. On Rosh Chodesh Iyar, 1937, I arrived at the address Moshe Binyomin had supplied in his letter to his father – the home of Reb Berele Katz at 15 Starre Mesta Street.

About a dozen other boys had received the same message. It was thrilling to be in the company of a whole group of students risking their lives to study Torah in secret.

Our Talmud teacher was Rabbi Moshe Rubinson (known as "Moshe Korolevitcher"), a wonderful personality and true Chossid, beloved by G-d and his fellow beings, who spent all his time studying Torah and teaching it, yet in a quiet manner that called no attention to himself. He was

Rabbi Berel Gurevitch, our Mashpiya for Chassidus studies

Reb Yisroel Levin, supervisor of our Yeshiva in Krivoy-Rog

renowned for his good heart, empathizing with the suffering of others as if it were his own.

Rabbi Berel Gurevitch (now head of the Beth Rivkah girls school in Paris, France) taught us "Chassidus" – Chabad philosophy.

This study was new to me and it impressed me deeply. Until today I remember the first Maamar (discourse) we studied, which began "Odom ki yakriv..." in the Alter Rebbe's work Likkutei Torah.

Those were happy times. For one, I was finally free of the embarrassment of having to eat every day at different homes. In Berditchev, each student received a few coins daily to buy his own food during the day, while in the evening we all went together to a place previously agreed upon to eat a warm supper.

But above all, the very existence of the Yeshiva in such dark times was a source of boundless joy. We knew we had to cherish every moment, and felt how every extra day we were able to learn Torah was a gift from G-d more precious than gold.

Unfortunately, that happy period of my life lasted just one month. News about the new Yeshiva spread and other students joined. The Yeshiva's heads, realizing they would be unable to keep so many students in one town, decided to open another branch of the Yeshiva elsewhere. I was among those selected to go.

KRIVOY-ROG

We were sent to Krivoy-Rog, about 350 kilometers from Berditchev. There were only four or five of us: Hirshel "the Breslover," Velvel Averbach, Mottel Levin (not Reb Yisroel Neveler's son) and I. Leibel Motchkin was with us for part of the time and Shmulik, son of Reb Yoel Itkin, the local Shochet (ritual slaughterer), joined us for studies.

In charge of the Yeshiva was a senior student, Yisroel Levin (known as "Yisroel Lippovitzer," who lives now in Kfar Chabad – father of Rabbi Sholom DovBer Levin, librarian of the central Lubavitch library at 770).

Everything had to be absolutely secret. Those were dangerous times and the local Torah-observant Jews were mortally afraid for a Yeshiva to exist in their city. Only the Shamash (attendant) of the Shul was aware of its existence. At night we slept in our own apartment. Early every

Krivoy-Rog: Karl Marx Street

morning, before the congregants arrived, we would go to the Shul and hide in the ladies' gallery – which was empty during the week – until prayers were over and everyone left.

When the Shamash locked the door from outside, it was the signal to emerge from our hiding place and go down into the men's section to study undisturbed for the rest of the day.

Sometimes we would go to the home of the Shochet, Reb Yoel Itkin, for a Chassidic Farbrengen (special Chassidic gathering).

It took just one month for the congregants to discover our secret. An uproar broke loose and they demanded that the Yeshiva leave, for it could get them into real trouble and might be used as an excuse for closing the Shul. We had to leave town.

DNIEPROPETROVSK

Together with Mottel Levin, I was sent to Dniepropetrovsk, not far from Krivoy-Rog. Here too we were warned against having contact with the local Jews so that the Yeshiva could remain secret. Here too we would hide in the ladies' gallery before the congregants arrived, going down to the Shul to study only after prayers were over.

On Shabbos, when women came to pray in the ladies' gallery, we had to hide in a side room in utter silence through the course of the long Shabbos service.

From our vantage point in the ladies' gallery, we had the privilege occasionally to see the Rabbi of the city, the renowned Torah giant and Kabbalist, Rabbi Levi Yitzchok

The Great Shul of Dniepropetrovsk, which the Soviets converted for secular use

Schneerson (1878-1944), father of our Rebbe. However, those in charge took care to avoid any contact between him and us, to prevent any risk to him.

In charge of our Yeshiva was Reb Sholom Vilenkin (who later lived in Nachalas Har Chabad at Kiryat Malachi in Israel). He was the son of the local Shochet, Rabbi Shneur Zalman Vilenkin, who had been privileged to be the Rebbe's teacher in his youth. Reb Sholom taught us and supplied us with all our needs, so that we were in relative comfort during our two months there.

Meanwhile, Krivoy-Rog had calmed down, so it was decided that we return there. We arrived back during the month of Elul and studied there until after the Tishrei holidays. But then the Yeshiva was discovered again and an uproar broke loose once more. We escaped to Dniepropetrovsk for a while, then back again to Krivoy-Rog when it calmed down.

Rabbi Shneur Zalman Vilenkin, who taught our Rebbe in his youth

Reb Sholom Vilenkin, our teacher in Dniepropetrovsk

The Great Shul today, restored to its original holiness. The view is from the ladies' gallery where we used to hide and study

By the third time we had to escape to Dniepropetrovsk, it was wintery weather, which is extremely cold in Ukraine. Having nowhere else to stay, I was forced to sleep at night in the Shul, a large cavernous building with no heat at night. The cold was bone-chilling. With no blanket, I would curl up in my coat, squeezing myself as small as possible so that it covered most of me, and try to doze off. I was only fourteen, and I shivered not just in cold but in fright; I was scared to sleep all alone through the long winter night in such a dark and spooky big building.

After a few days, however, we received a message to return to Krivoy-Rog. When we got there, Yisroel informed us regretfully that it was no longer possible to maintain a Yeshiva in the town, and we would have to go to other

Rabbi Levi Yitzchok Schneerson, Chief Rabbi of Yekaterinoslav-Dniepropetrovsk, father of our Rebbe

branches of the Yeshiva. He gave each of us a destination and we set out on our various ways.

KLINTZE

The destination I was given was Klintze in White Russia, the home of Rabbi Yosef Goldberg (known as "Yoske Tiraspoler"). Already then he had a reputation as an outstanding Talmudic scholar (later he served for many decades as Rosh Yeshiva of Yeshivas Tomchei Tmimim Lubavitch in Brunoy near Paris, France).

Reb Yosef received me warmly. But he explained that he already had four students, and teaching more than four could be dangerous. (Apparently, in order to avoid the increasing risk, the Rebbe had instructed that the Yeshiva be split into groups of four students.) His four students were also older than I and more advanced.

Nevertheless, he told me to stay with him meanwhile, for I had nowhere else to go. Every morning he would leave to teach his students, while I had to stay at home, for it was too risky for me to leave the house. It was like being under house-arrest. I tried to study on my own, but spent most of the time reading Tehilim (Psalms) in tears.

After a short while, Reb Yosef told me there was no point in my staying with him any longer. He suggested I go to Starodub, to Rabbi Zalman Shimon Dworkin (later the respected Rabbi of Crown Heights, Brooklyn, New York), who worked by day at a government-owned plant in the nearby town of Nietche, but could teach me at night.

STARODUB

Rabbi Zalman Katzenelenbogen (now Kazen), in his youth

In Starodub, I was overjoyed to find another Yeshiva student, Reb Zalman Katzenelenbogen (later abbreviated to Kazen, who now lives in Cleveland, Ohio). Now I had someone of my own age as a study-partner and companion.

But there, too, we found no rest. One day, as I sat studying in Shul together with Zalman, Rebbetzin Dworkin suddenly came to see us.

She was crying. The secret police had come to their home asking about her husband. Luckily they had not noticed a letter that had arrived just that day for Zalman, for she had placed it on top of a closet to give him later. After they left, she saw that it was from Zalman's mother, renowned as the "Mumeh Sorke" – "Aunt Soroh."

She decided to read it in case it contained an urgent message.

Indeed it did: His mother had written that the secret police had arrested his father, Reb Michoel, so Zalman could not return home but should go into hiding immediately wherever he was able...

Rebbetzin Dworkin had to leave at once for Nietche, where her husband worked, to alert him of the danger and make sure he did not return home where he would likely be arrested.

She asked me to accompany her. I remember the scene as if it happened today: It was raining outside, but even more tears flowed from the Rebbetzin's eyes, for she was afraid we would miss her husband. Thank G-d, we found him and he left town immediately, succeeding in escaping the police.

That night we stayed in Nietche at the home of the Shochet, and returned next morning to Starodub. But now I had no reason to stay longer and I returned to Rabbi Yosef Goldberg in Klintze.

Again I went through a difficult time, spending my days in tears, reading Tehilim. Desperately I prayed to G-d to be able to return to Berditchev where I had so enjoyed studying.

Rabbi Zalman Shimon Dworkin, later Rabbi of the central Lubavitcher community, Crown Heights

Finally, at the beginning of Kislev (end of 1937), Reb Yosef suggested that since there was no study program for me in Klintze, I should return to Berditchev. He pointed out that Reb Moshe Rubinson was so kindhearted that, when he would hear of all my wanderings and sufferings over the past seven months, he would surely accept me back.

BACK TO BERDITCHEV

Reb Yosef gave me money for my train fare and I traveled back to Berditchev. Sure enough, as soon as Reb Moshe heard my story, he agreed to accept me. "After suffering so much," he said, "you should stay here. Whatever will be our lot will be yours, too..."

My joy was boundless. Finally I had a place to study again, without having to wander from place to place. After Reb Moshe's Talmud lesson, I would go with my study-partner, Sholom Ber Pewzner (brother of Rabbi Hillel Pewzner, now Rabbi of the Lubavitcher community of Paris), to the Chevra Mishnayos Shul to review it.

BERDITCHEV WAS DIFFERENT

The years 1937 to 1939 were the darkest period of Soviet Communism. Hardly a family in the USSR was untouched by the purges and mass arrests. The regime arrested all the Torah-observant Jews it could find, especially Lubavitcher and Breslover Chassidim who were known to be the most dedicated and active in preserving Jewish life. Many were liquidated within a short time, while most of the others were cruelly tortured and condemned to long sentences in remote labor camps in the gulags from where few returned.

Many Breslover Chassidim lived in Uman, where my family still lived. One night, the police arrested all Breslover men without exception, sending all off to labor camps where most eventually died. Father was not home

One of Berditchev's many Shuls

then and escaped their fate, thank G-d.

In Berditchev, however, Yiddishkeit still flourished. At a time when most Shuls in the USSR had been forcibly closed, leaving many large cities without a single Shul, Berditchev's Shuls were open and full of Jewish life. I remember eighteen Shuls in the town, and there may have

Rabbi Sholom Shachna Friedman with his three sons, Dovid, Meir and Mordechai

been more.

It is difficult to adequately describe the warm, vibrant Jewish atmosphere and holiness of Berditchev. Reb Berele Katz, for example, a Boyaner Chossid, was a dwarf in stature but wonderfully lively and incomparably kindhearted. On Shabbos he would spend many hours in prayer, staying long after everyone had left, praying slowly and in song just like a Lubavitcher "Oved" (one who "works" upon himself and prays slowly with deep devotion).

Another impressive personality was Rabbi Sholom Shachna Friedman, direct descendant of the renowned Ruzhiner Rebbe, Rabbi Yisroel Friedman (1796-1850, great-grandson of the Maggid of Mezeritch). He was so handsome and dignified that people would stop in the street just to watch him as he walked by. His brothers also served as Rabbis: Rabbi Zushe in Odessa and Rabbi Yankele in Kiev (he was the father of Reb Aharon Friedman and Reb Meir Friedman, both now in Kfar Chabad, and Rabbi Yisroel Friedman, Rosh Yeshiva of Oholei Torah, Crown Heights, Brooklyn).

Rabbi Sholom's three sons were all special:

Dovidel, the eldest, was brilliant, with an astounding memory.

He once asked me to test him on the Talmudic tractate Bava Kamma, which he was studying: "Open the Gemara wherever you like, read a few words aloud, and I'll continue by heart."

It was no idle boast: Wherever I read, he continued with the Gemara's exact words, for he had learned the whole tractate by heart, word by word!

His second son, Meirel, just seven years old, was also a gifted child who studied assiduously. But most memorable of all was little Mottele, who was only five. Before Shabbos, he would stand on a bench in Shul to read through Shir Hashirim (the Song of Songs) – as many have the custom to do – reading it aloud in such a sweet voice that just watching him was a pure spiritual delight!

CHAPTER FIVE

CHILDREN IN JAIL

FARBRENGEN

Almost two months passed, busy in study. I was overjoyed to be back in a full Yeshiva atmosphere in the company of other students.

There were about eight of us, six of my age level and two older.

On 24 Teves – the anniversary of the passing of the Alter Rebbe in 1812 – our teachers decided to mark the occasion by holding a Farbrengen (special Chassidic gathering) at the Tailors' Shul. We washed our hands to eat bread, and sat down to a meal of potatoes and herring. Singing the hauntingly beautiful Chabad melodies, we wished each other the traditional "L'chayim" blessing on little glasses of Mashkeh (alcohol), as is customary.

After each round of spirited song, both our teachers told us stories of great saintly personalities and Chassidim of past generations, inspiring us to serve G-d with total acceptance and obey His commands unquestioningly. Reb Moshe explained at length how King Shaul had sinned and fallen from his high spiritual level because he based his service of G-d purely on intellect, which is limited. He urged us to keep the Yeshiva schedule conscientiously and cherish every moment of Torah study.

We drank in every word thirstily. It was an exalted and inspiring evening.

UNINVITED GUESTS

Suddenly, between one and two in the morning, the calm of the night was disturbed by mighty blows at the front door. Reb Moshe and Reb Berel immediately dashed into a side room where wood was stacked for the furnace, hiding between the logs.

The front door crashed open and in burst two policemen, their revolvers at the ready in their hands. But the sight they encountered was considered innocent enough in those days – a group of teenaged boys sitting around a bottle of vodka! They stared at us and were about to leave, when one insisted on making a thorough search.

It did not take them long to discover our teachers' hiding place.

"What are you doing here?" they demanded to know.

"We were just passing by," our teachers explained, "when we noticed the light on in the Shul. We came in and found these boys eating a meal, so we asked to join them."

But the police did not accept that excuse. Later we realized that they had been aware of our Yeshiva, and for a

The author, before his arrest

long time had been awaiting the right moment to catch us in organized study.

They ordered us to line up and march to the police station in single file. The Shamash of the Shul, who had been sitting in the hallway, was ordered to join the line. One of the police led the line and the other followed behind us.

At first we were somewhat relieved that we were being taken to the police station, rather than the headquarters of the dreaded secret police. That gave us some hope that it would be easier for us to escape.

However, after spending the rest of the night at the police station, we were ordered the next morning onto a special truck used for transporting convicts. With us sat two policemen, their guns at the ready in their hands. We were told to keep our heads down; apparently the police did not feel comfortable transporting young boys through the streets of the town in a convict truck! The truck drove off... straight for the secret police headquarters! Now we realized we would not be able to leave so fast...

"NO TZITZIS?"

Except for the chief, Berditchev's secret police officers were all Jewish and familiar with Jewish observances. When we arrived, they took away our Tefilin. Maliciously, one of them cut off the Tzitzis fringes hanging from all four corners of our Talis Kottons (rectangular garments worn by Jewish males to fulfill the commandment of Tzitzis continuously). We had no choice but to take off our Talis Kottons immediately, for male Jews may not wear a four-cornered garment unless all corners have kosher Tzitzis.

But those police officers soon came to regret what they had done. After coming into the building, we were ordered into the yard to have our pictures taken from all angles. Suddenly one of the superior officers asked: "Where are your Tzitzis? What kind of Cheder is this without Tzitzis?" He told us to make our Tzitzis noticeable. We told him the policemen had cut them off, so we had to take off our Talis Kottons.

He turned livid with rage, yelling at the policemen for their thoughtlessness: "If they have no Tzitzis," he screamed, "how are we supposed to prove that this is a Cheder?"

Maybe they wanted to use our pictures as proof against us, or perhaps they hoped to use them in their propaganda abroad to give the impression that there was freedom of religion in the Soviet Union and that even Torah schools still existed.

While the photographer was busy taking our pictures, the officer suddenly asked the Shamash of the Shul: "Is the Torah teacher a good one? Does he teach well?"

The Shamash, who wasn't the smartest fellow, fell right into his trap: "Oh, yes," he answered, "he's really exceptional!"

We all broke out in a cold sweat. But although we were terrified, we all remained determined to keep to our story without letting out a word about the Yeshiva's existence, even if it meant we would have to suffer for it terribly.

INTERROGATION

One by one we were called in for our first interrogation. Each of us was asked his name, address, age and occupation.

My interrogator was a Jew named Khutaretsky. I gave my parents' address. Although I was already close to fifteen and certainly didn't look like an eleven-year-old, I gave the age stated on my identification document – eleven!

"Liar!" shot back the interrogator.

But I stuck to my story: "Why are you calling me a liar? I don't know what you want of me. I'm only eleven."

"What chutzpa," he raged, "telling me such an obvious lie with a straight face!"

After a while he calmed down and started asking me all sorts of ordinary questions.

"Do you put on Tefilin every day?" he asked suddenly.

"Of course," I replied, caught off guard.

He crashed his fist down on the table. "See how you're lying!" he yelled. "How do you dare to tell me you're only eleven when you're really past Bar-Mitzva?"

Composing myself, I replied calmly: "We're allowed to put on Tefilin starting at the age of eleven."

"Liar!" he screamed, boiling with rage. "I'll show you!"

He pressed his bell. "Bring in Rubinson," he ordered.

When my teacher entered, Khutaretsky asked him: "Rabbi, from what age does one start putting on Tefilin?"

Realizing why he was asking, my teacher replied shrewdly:

"According to the Torah, we have the obligation to start from the age of thirteen. But our Sages allow us to start from the age of eleven..."

The interrogator knew we were misleading him, and he was fuming. But since I was so stubborn and my official documents actually supported me, it was not worth pressing the point further.

However, this friction right at the start made me suffer much more than my fellow students. Either way: If indeed I was lying, it was reason enough to pressure me endlessly. On the other hand, if I really was the youngest, then I must be the weakest link in the group, and much more susceptible to pressure for information that would be more difficult to squeeze out of the others.

Khutaretsky pressed me hard to admit the existence of the underground Cheder. But I denied it vehemently: "What Cheder? What teacher? Who wants to study all day anyway? I ran away from home and came here to earn a few pennies. I happened to pass by and met a few friends, joining them for a shot of vodka..." That was my story and I stuck to it.

We were interrogated relentlessly through the day until the evening, when we were sent to our cells. Our teachers Reb Moshe and Reb Berel, together with the two older students, Eliezer Mogilevsky and Shmuel Itkin, were placed together in one cell, while we younger ones were sent to a different one. With me were Velvel Averbach, Sholom Ber Pewzner, Refoel Wilschanski, Heschel Tzeitlin and Refoel Brook (unlike the rest of us, after World War II he stayed behind in the USSR where he passed away recently. After the collapse of the Soviet Union, he yearned to see the Rebbe but feared that just setting eyes on him would make him pass out from deep emotion).

The cell was a long one, with bunks along the side for sleeping. These were already all taken by other prisoners, most of whom were Jewish. The only place left was under the bunks, where we managed to lie down for our night's sleep.

HUNGER AND THIRST

During our four weeks in jail we suffered terribly from hunger. Except for bread, no other food served at the jail was kosher. But the bread was so dry and foul-tasting that at first we were reluctant to eat it.

Our jailers told us: "Boys, eat the bread, because even that won't be enough to satisfy your hunger." Indeed, we

Refoel Wilschanski, after leaving the Soviet Union

Velvel Averbach, after leaving the Soviet Union

soon started to starve. Every morning, pieces of bread were distributed which were far from enough for a meal. At lunch they gave out soup, which was not kosher, of course, so we ate nothing. It is impossible to describe our constant hunger pangs.

Another problem was thirst. Our cell was very hot, so we were always thirsty for water. The water given to the inmates was barely enough to quench everyone's thirst. But we also needed much more for washing our hands ("Negel Vasser") every morning on arising and before eating bread. Our cellmates, however, were upset with what they considered this waste of the precious water allotted to us, and decided that each should get only a regular fixed share.

It was very hard to get by on that limited amount of water. We were forced to make our morning hand-washing double for our meal of bread, too. On awaking in the morning, we would wash our hands, saying the blessing "Al

Heschel Tzeitlin, after leaving the Soviet Union

Refoel Brook, in his older years

netilas yodoyim," then the other morning blessings, and immediately afterward the blessing for bread, "Hamotzi lechem min ho'oretz." After that we would recite our morning prayers. Otherwise we would not have had enough extra water to wash again before eating the bread, which was our only meal of the day. Through the rest of the day and night, we starved and thirsted.

THREATS AND ENTICEMENTS

The interrogations intensified. Again and again we were summoned for interrogation at all times of the day or night. They grilled us relentlessly back and forth, trying to find out who was organizing the Yeshiva. We denied everything, all presenting the same story: We were just a group of boys who liked to get together now and then for a drink and enjoy ourselves.

One evening, around dusk, I was summoned to an interrogation.

That interrogation remains in my mind to this day like a nightmare.

It was winter, so it was still early in the evening.

Khutaretsky grilled me, hour upon hour, till around midnight.

Although I was absolutely terrified, I stuck to my story: I didn't know anything about a Cheder, I didn't know what he wanted of me, and I was only eleven years old. Whatever I said, he shot back "Liar!" He was burning with rage, threatening that he would "show me yet" so that I would come to regret my lies.

After a few days, I was summoned again at nightfall. It was a repeat performance – the same questions, the same denials, the same threats. This time, however, someone new was present. Introducing himself as the local school principal, he spoke to me nicely:

"You look like a smart boy who understands what we're telling you. Why are you acting so foolishly, doing yourself such harm that you have to rot here in these jail cells? It's smarter to confess and give them the information they want. Then you'll be released, and they'll give you nice clothes to wear instead of these rags."

He spoke to me for hours, promising me the world. Soon, I thought, he would offer to make me Czar of Russia...

I just ignored everything he said, making no comment at all.

Suddenly, one of them – I don't remember whether the principal or Khutaretsky – said to the other: "Let me tell you a story about one of the Rabbi Schneersohns and Napoleon." He started telling the well-known story of the renowned Chossid Rabbi Moshe Meisels, who was sent by the Alter Rebbe to spy on the French army when Napoleon invaded Russia in 1812. Napoleon suspected him and once suddenly placed his hand upon Reb Moshe's heart to feel whether it was beating uncontrollably from fear. But Reb Moshe had such control over himself that his heartbeat remained normal. Later he explained that the Alter Rebbe's teaching, that the mind rules over the heart, a teaching that he succeeded in integrating into his personality, had saved him from certain death.

He told the story well, slowly and vividly. At first I could not fathom why all of a sudden he was telling such a story in the middle of the interrogation. But soon I noticed that, while telling it, his eyes didn't leave me for a moment. Instinctively, I realized I had better be careful.

On and on the story went, while he continued staring at me.

Suddenly I realized what he wanted. He was watching me to see any reaction that might reveal that I knew the story. Then he could start a new round of interrogation, for how does an eleven-year-old know such a story?

Actually I had heard the story. But I took care to show no recognition, staring back at him with innocent eyes as if this was the first time I was hearing it...

Seeing that their ruse had failed, the interrogator went back to grilling me. But soon his patience burst: "I've had enough of this already!" he yelled. "I can't play games with you any more! I've got no time for this! It has to stop immediately! Nothing will help you; you've got to tell me everything!"

"What do you want of me?" I insisted. "I don't know anything about it."

Finally, he warned: "Listen, if you confess, good. If not, you'll be beaten to death right here on the spot!"

He pressed his bell. A non-Jewish ruffian came in holding a thick leather whip with thin straps affixed to one end (a "cat o'nine tails").

I was horrified. I knew what such lashes meant. A non-Jewish cellmate of ours summoned to an interrogation one night had returned the next morning with his face sickly pale, as white as chalk. Pulling up his shirt, he had shown us how his flesh was covered with bright red welts and black and blue bruises from lashes with a whip just like this.

Such sights were common in the jail and they terrified everyone. The interrogators did not hesitate to inflict the cruellest tortures. As children, however, we had hoped to remain safe from torture.

"Get up and pull down your pants!" he ordered.

I remember that moment as if it were today. My knees were knocking uncontrollably. With trembling fingers, I started trying to undo my buttons.

It seemed to take an eternity. But then he barked again: "Sit down!" Even after I sat down, my knees were still shaking so hard that all efforts could not keep them still.

The hours went by. Khutaretsky tormented me ceaselessly, with ominous threats calculated to break my spirit. Suddenly he announced that he was phoning to Uman. He spoke a few words into his telephone receiver and told me: "I have just phoned the secret police in Uman to arrest your mother and bring her here."

By two or three in the morning, I was utterly exhausted.

"You must be hungry?" he asked me.

"Yes," I admitted.

Again he picked up the telephone receiver, calling the jail kitchen: "Bring food for a Jew who eats only kosher." A few moments later, a woman came in and set before me some bread and two boiled eggs. My eyes lit up. I didn't think then whether eggs not cooked by a Torah-observant Jew were kosher or not. Still, as eager as I was to eat, I didn't make a move.

"Oh, I know," said the interrogator. "You want to wash your hands before eating bread." He allowed me to wash and, after reciting the appropriate blessings, I quickly swallowed the food.

After I finished eating, he thought I would return his favor by cooperating. But I continued to deny everything. He went wild with rage, calling for the whip again to terrify me into changing my tune.

It was a night I will never forget. Only when it was close to four in the morning did he let me return to my cell. My head was swimming as if I were drunk, and I was so dizzy that I literally did not know what was happening to me.

REFUSING TO SIGN

A few days later, I was summoned again. Unexpectedly, Khutaretsky greeted me with a smile: "How are you, Chatzkel Brod? How are you doing?"

This time he changed his approach, trying to win me over by being friendly. He started telling me many stories. Soon I realized that he was trying again to see if they were familiar to me. If I was only eleven, I would not understand too much, but if it were obvious I understood, then I must be older. So I kept quiet and made no comment.

In the middle of his stories, he handed me a paper to sign. I refused. He took it back and continued. Then he tried again.

"I'm not signing anything," I told him.

Nothing else was helping, so he tried flattery, hoping to gain my confidence. He praised me to the sky, with all imaginable compliments. Then he handed me the paper again.

"No, I'm not going to sign anything," I insisted.

Seeing that flattery did not help, he tried another tack. He started promising me the world. There was nothing he didn't guarantee me that night. If half his promises had been fulfilled, I should have become one of the Soviet Union's greatest leaders...

Again he handed me the paper to sign. It listed names of Chassidim against whom my signature would be used as testimony.

In my mind rang the saying of the Talmud (Pesachim 25b): "Why is your blood considered redder [more important] than someone else's?" By signing, I would bring misfortune upon so many precious families. What right did I have to save my own skin by making others suffer? Again I refused. Finally, he said: "Listen, Brod. We've decided to release you. You're still a child and there is nothing to be done with you here.

"Now it is night, but tomorrow we'll give you money to travel home. Meanwhile, just sign this paper and tomorrow you'll be free."

However, with G-d's help I kept my word and did not sign or bring harm to any other Jews.

THE GAME IS OVER

One evening I was summoned to another interrogation.

This time my teacher Reb Moshe was present. He told me: "Listen, Chatzkel, you can confess now. I've told the interrogators that I was teaching you and taken the whole blame on myself. Now you can tell them the truth and bring this whole business to an end."

To me it seemed obvious that the interrogators had forced him to say that to get us to confess. So I looked at him as if I didn't know him and said: "You're lying! I don't know you, and I've never been taught by you!"

The interrogator exploded with rage: "Insolent child! How dare you refuse to obey what your teacher is telling you!"

Nothing helped. I stuck to my story that I knew nothing about any Cheder or Yeshiva. Later I learned that the interrogators got the same response when they brought Reb Moshe in to convince another of my fellow students to confess.

By this time, however, the interrogators were anxious to bring the whole episode to a conclusion. They sent Reb Moshe to stay in our cell so that we could talk freely. What he told us put an end to our resolve: "You can all confess that I was your teacher. I've taken responsibility upon myself for everything. Of course, don't tell them anything about who sent you here or who was supplying you with meals. About all that, continue saying that you know nothing..."

There was no reason any longer to continue our stubborn refusal to cooperate. We signed confessions and that was it.

JAIL SENTENCES

By accepting responsibility, Reb Moshe knew he would have to suffer for it. The secret police tried to blame him for other crimes, accusing him of illegal contacts with personalities abroad and helping to organize counter-revolutionary groups. They transferred him to a jail in Kiev, planning to try him at a public show-trial. But after about a year he was released, thank G-d.

Incredibly, he went right back to teaching in underground Yeshivos until his last day in the USSR. In 1946, Reb Moshe succeeded in leaving with the great Lubavitcher exodus from the Soviet Union, continuing to teach the refugee youth as they wandered across Europe. Unfortunately, on 24 Teves, 5709 (1949), exactly eleven years after our arrest, he passed away in Paris.

Rabbi Berel Gurevitch, in recent years

Reb Berel Gurevitch and the two older students, Eliezer Mogilevsky and Shmuel Itkin, were sentenced to a year in jail. The two students were released on 10 Kislev, the anniversary of the 1825 liberation from Czarist imprisonment of the second Chabad leader, the "Mitteler Rebbe," Rabbi DovBer of Lubavitch (1773-1827). Reb Berel was released a week later on 19 Kislev, the anniversary of the Alter Rebbe's 1798 liberation.

Reb Berel has written about his experiences ("Kfar Chabad" weekly #596), describing his Pesach in jail and his interrogators' efforts to force him to eat food containing leaven (which Jews are forbidden to eat on Passover). In jail he was beaten mercilessly.

When that didn't help, his hands were held behind him in an effort to force-feed him. But just when the spoon of soup was pushed into his mouth, he coughed with all his might, blowing the soup straight into his interrogator's face. That put an end to their efforts...

In jail we met Rabbi Sholom Friedman, who was arrested with Reb Berele Katz some time after our own arrest. Later we learned that, from the day of our arrest, Rabbi Friedman had refused to sleep in bed: "How can I lie down to sleep when young boys are in jail for studying Torah?" The police who came to arrest him found him awaiting them fully clothed and ready to go. Apparently he expected to be arrested (as were most Torah-observant Jews at the time) but knew of no place to where he could escape. I believe he passed away in jail.

RELEASE

On Friday, 26 Shvat, 5698 (1938), guards came into our cell and started reading out names. Whoever was called, had to take his belongings and leave the cell.

One of the prisoners left behind a piece of bread. We were so hungry that my fellow-student Sholom Ber Pewzner crawled over to grab it. But a non-Jewish ruffian beat him to it, pushing him so violently that we were sure he must have broken his bones. So hungry was Sholom Ber that he jumped right back to attack the non-Jew and retrieve that piece of bread. We had to restrain him by force to keep him away!

After everyone else was called out of the cell, our names were also called and we were told to leave. We were taken into a car and ordered again to keep our heads down – the police were embarrassed that boys would be seen being transported in a police vehicle...

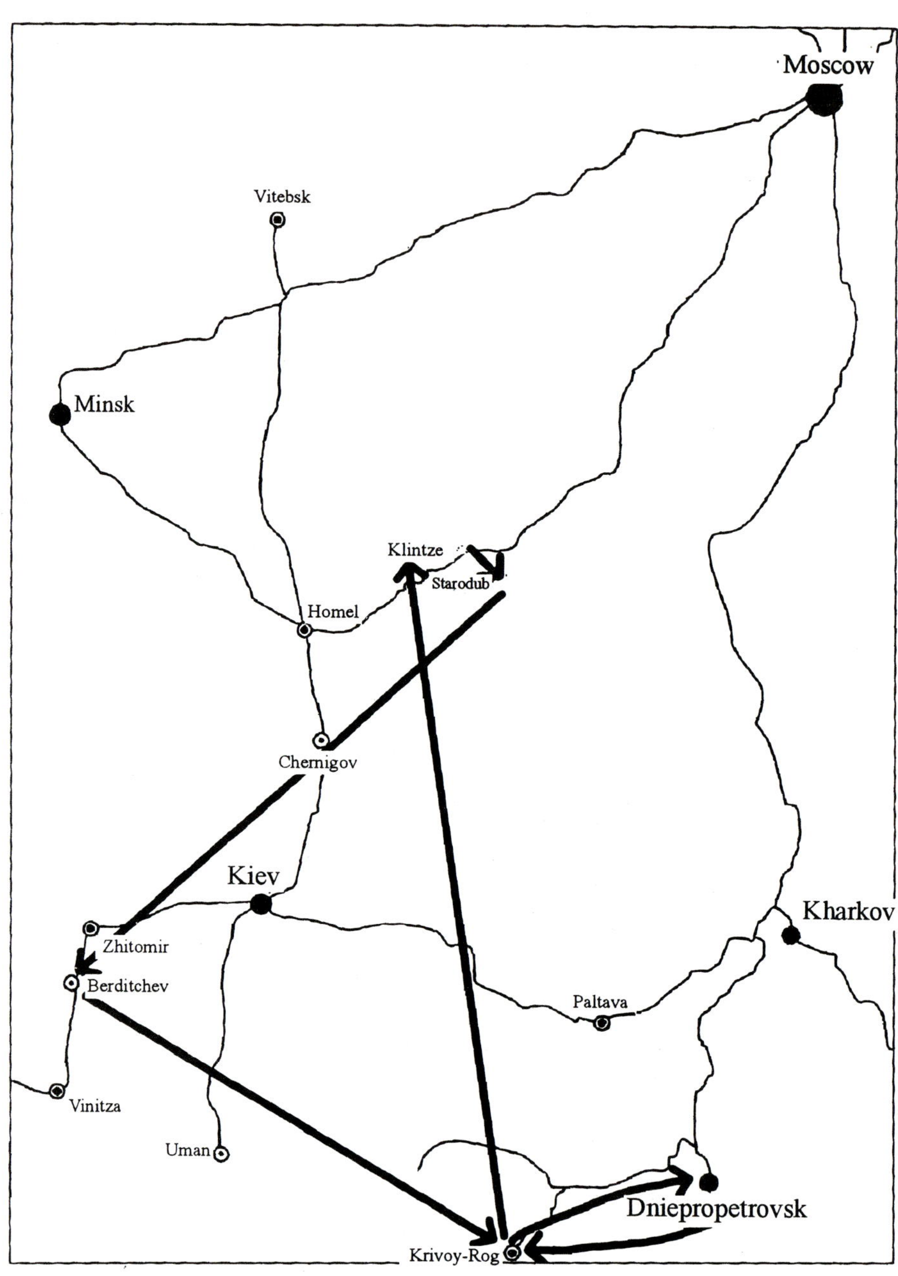

Wanderings: From Berditchev to Krivoy-Rog, to Dniepropetrovsk, back to Krivoy-Rog, to Klintze, to Staradub then back to Berditchev

CHAPTER SIX

THE ORPHANAGE

KEEPING SHABBOS

We were taken to a government orphanage. It was an impressive place, set among beautiful greenery. We could tell it had once belonged to Jews because the doorposts showed marks of Mezuzos that had been removed. There was even a Sukkah on the grounds with its S'chach – temporary roof of branches – still intact.

This orphanage was for children who had had one parent arrested, while the other was unable to take care of them. Most of the children were Jewish, as was the director himself. By order of Stalin, such orphanages were established throughout the Soviet Union to brainwash the children of people arrested for political and religious "crimes."

We were led into the spacious dining room, where the tables were set with food and drink. The principal gave us a special speech: "Welcome! Now you are no longer under the jurisdiction of the secret police. You are free. But here you have to keep the rules of this institution. You may not leave without permission, you must take off your hats, and you must eat whatever you are served." He continued with a list of other rules.

Of course, our hats stayed on...

It was Friday, the eve of Shabbos, and we took the opportunity to bathe ourselves for the first time since we had been jailed. Our bodies were thick with over a month's dirt and perspiration. We were given new underclothes and already started to feel better.

On Friday evening, when Shabbos began, we prayed the Shabbos prayers by heart together, then went into the dining room. What a sight! There was bread in abundance! We pushed aside the non-kosher food and piled up bread in front of us. Children from other tables around us gave us more bread. We washed our hands, said the Kiddush blessings to sanctify the Shabbos and sat down to eat.

That night, a few of us, myself included, suffered terrible stomach-aches. Our stomachs had so contracted from lack of food that they could not digest so much bread...

The school administration did not appreciate our religious observance that Shabbos. Repeatedly they told us to take off our hats, but we refused. By Sunday they decided we were not suitable for their orphanage.

FROM ORPHANAGE TO ORPHANAGE

A police officer arrived and told us we were being transferred to another orphanage. We complained why we had to be in an orphanage at all, for we had parents of our own and wished to return home.

But the policeman told us: "We can't rely on you. You'll get together somewhere else and start studying again in an unlawful Cheder. You need to be reeducated."

We were taken by car about ten kilometers outside town. This government orphanage, also very attractive, was for children whose parents had both passed away or been arrested. The principal, a non-Jew, gave us the same impressive speech as the previous one.

TEFILIN IN THE FOREST

What troubled us most was that we had no Tefilin. In jail, of course, we could not even think about it. But now we had more freedom and were trying to find some way to get hold of a pair.

We met with the principal and told him we lacked the most minimal personal belongings, as everything had been left behind in Berditchev, and we asked permission for two of us to go into town to get them for us. He gave his permission, and the two boys managed to obtain kosher butter and other kosher foods that allowed us to vary our all-bread menu.

Best of all, they brought back the greatest treasure – a pair of Tefilin! Now we had to find a quiet place where we could put them on unnoticed.

It was the middle of the winter and the local lakes were frozen over. We told the principal that after a month in jail we badly needed exercise. Could we go ice-skating? He

The holy resting place of the renowned Rabbi Levi Yitzchok in Berditchev

gave his permission, and off we went with skates to one of the lakes.

In the surrounding forest, we found a concealed place where we took turns putting on the Tefilin.

After over a month of being unable to fulfill that exalted Mitzva, it is impossible to describe the joy of those moments. With tears in our eyes we held the Tefilin lovingly, and it was difficult for each of us to take them off to give the next boy his chance.

At the same time, we used the opportunity to visit Berditchev's Jewish cemetery, where we prayed at the grave of the famed Rabbi of Berditchev, Rabbi Levi Yitzchok

(1740-1809). We wrote and read a Pidyon Nefesh (request that he intercede for us in Heaven), begging tearfully that he arouse Divine mercy upon us to escape from the hands of the government officials and reach some place where we could study Torah again.

We made this a daily habit, obtaining permission to go ice-skating, putting on Tefilin in the forest and visiting Rabbi Levi Yitzchok's grave.

ESCAPE PLANS

A few weeks later, we asked again and received permission for two of us to go into town. Walking through the streets, the two were surprised to meet Michoel Teitelbaum, (now in Brooklyn, where he has established the respected Oholei Torah-Oholei Menachem Yeshivos for 1,500 students of all ages, may G-d grant him a full and speedy recovery).

Michoel's face was wrapped in a bandage to hide his beard, but the boys recognized him immediately. He signaled them to follow him as he entered a Shul and went up to the ladies' gallery. After greeting them warmly and asking how all the boys were, he told them to start working on an escape plan.

Reb Michoel had come to Berditchev from Zhitomir, where there was a Chassidic community. One Chossid named Reb Mordechai Leizer, when he had heard about our arrest and confinement in the orphanage, had told Michoel: "Whatever happens to us, we have the duty to save these boys!" They were especially alarmed to hear a report that we were being kept in the company of unsavory non-Jews, making it even more urgent to get us out.

The boys told him that we had heard from other children at the orphanage that the administration was unhappy with our disobedience of the rules and continued religious conduct, and had decided to transfer us to another orphanage sixty kilometers away, past Tchernigov, in a location far from any habitation, where the administration could handle us better. We did not know when this transfer was to take place, but it was clearly necessary to get us out as soon as possible.

Carefully we planned our escape. The only day in the week when it would be somewhat easier was Shabbos, when the principal stayed home and we were watched much less closely. We agreed on the details of the plan, which we hoped to carry out the following Shabbos. (In a case such as ours that involved saving Jewish lives in the spiritual sense by keeping us within the Torah-observant Jewish community, Torah law necessitates breaking the Shabbos.)

A TEARFUL MEETING

That Friday, I was told that someone awaited me outside.

I went out and my heart skipped a beat: My Mother was standing there! Somehow she had learned of our whereabouts and had come to visit me.

Our meeting was very painful and emotional. We cried bitterly at my unfortunate situation. Tears choked Mother's throat to see her son confined in an orphanage with no way of getting him out.

Of course, I could not tell her about our escape plan, but I tried to calm her: "Mother, go home and don't worry. Soon I'll be released, with G-d's help. But I can't go home anyway. I'll go to Moscow and try to find a place where I can continue studying Torah."

She burst into bitter tears: "Chatzkele, dear, you see how much you're suffering. They might tear you away from Jews and Judaism altogether. Better stay home, where you'll grow up a Torah-observant Jew."

"Mother, you know I can't promise you that I'll come home. Trust in G-d. He won't forsake us."

Mother left, crushed and brokenhearted, wondering when

Rabbi Michoel Teitelbaum. standing at right: Rabbi Moshe Marozov

she would ever see her son again...

FREEDOM!

Shabbos came. We were given permission to go ice-skating, and left separately in pairs so as not to arouse suspicion.

Once we were all out, we went to the agreed-upon meeting place with Michoel. We had a little scare when one of the boys told us he had seen the principal driving his car in the direction of the orphanage. Nevertheless, we decided to proceed with our plan. Michoel gave us train tickets, and each pair took the train to a different destination.

My partner was Heschel Tzeitlin, who had an aunt in Homel (Gomel), White Russia. We arrived there on Sunday at midday. Later we heard that the other boys had also reached their destinations successfully.

Altogether we had spent about six weeks at the orphanage.

CHAPTER SEVEN

JOURNEY INTO THE UNKNOWN

MOSCOW

Going home to Uman was out of the question. I had given the police my address there, and it would be the first place they would look for me. I decided to go to Moscow where Father was staying, although I had no idea where.

On Monday I left Homel for Moscow. To find out Father's whereabouts, I went to the Shul. A Lubavitcher noticed me there and walked by without looking at me, whispering: "What are you doing here? Get out of here immediately!"

I understood. He had my safety in mind. During those frightful months, thousands of Chabad and other Chassidim were arrested, many never to be heard of again. It was dangerous for anyone to be seen in a Shul, certainly someone young.

Meanwhile, Father found out I was in town and located me. He arranged a place for me to stay and eat. But I was

Red Square, Moscow

still neither here nor there. Where would I be for Pesach, which was but a few weeks away? Where would I study and find a more permanent refuge?

In Moscow lived a Chossid renowned for his life of Mesiras Nefesh, Reb Yonah Kagan (Cohen), who was in charge of funding the various branches of Yeshivas Tomchei Tmimim. When referring to him, everyone called him by a false name, "Reb Shillem," so that if students or others were arrested and forced to reveal who was supporting the Yeshiva, they would not know his real name.

(Reb Yonah managed to evade arrest long after most other Chabad Chassidim. Eventually the secret police caught up with him in the late 1940's. He would not eat

bread baked by non-Jews, and even in jail demanded that Jewish-baked bread be brought in for him. Under such conditions, there was little chance of surviving in a Soviet jail. He was condemned to hard labor and passed away in prison camp, leaving no children, but remembered with reverence by the many Chassidim for whom he gave his life.)

One day I saw Reb Yonah at Shul and wanted to tell him my problem. However, it seemed he was aware of my situation and knew he could not help me. When I tried to approach him, he avoided me and left. I understood. But what was I to do now?

However, Reb Yonah was not giving up on me. At that time a senior student several years older than I, Nochum Wolosow (now in Crown Heights), was in Moscow. He was

Moscow: The train terminal to Gruzia is at the left

in contact with Reb Yonah, and together they considered my options. Nochum informed Father that I could travel to Kutais, Gruzia (Soviet Georgia), where a branch of Tomchei Tmimim was in process of formation.

Father asked if I wanted to go. It was no simple decision. Kutais was in the Caucasus, 1,700 kilometers from Moscow and over three days journey by train. I knew nothing about the land, nor whether its residents even knew the Russian language so that I could communicate with them. For a boy not yet fifteen, it was frightening to travel so far away into the unknown. Yet there seemed to be no other choice.

Father bought me a train ticket, new clothes and essentials, for all my belongings had been left behind in Berditchev.

A Soviet locomotive

FAREWELL TO FATHER

Together we took the subway to the railroad terminal. When we reached the stop for the terminal, I begged Father not to accompany me upstairs for fear of his being noticed by the police.

Constant fear pervaded our lives, especially during that dark period when so many people were arrested. Just the sight of a uniformed policeman was enough to send shudders down the spine. Besides uniformed police, there were secret police agents everywhere, watching everyone and everything for the slightest suspicion. People were arrested constantly, and forced to submit to relentless interrogation and often torture.

Father's beard and Peyos were enough reason to arrest him. Walking with a young boy through the train terminal – which was swarming with police and agents interested in who was coming and going – would make him seem even more suspicious.

As painful as it would be not to have Father accompany me all the way to the train, I insisted on saying goodbye there at the subway station. Although I felt like bursting into tears, and Father must have felt the same, we managed to control ourselves not to show it outwardly. Neither of us knew when, if ever, we would see each other again. Only many years later, after I had children of my own, was I able to appreciate what Father must have felt at that moment. But I was able to feel my own sharp pain.

TEFILIN ON THE TRAIN

Young as I was, I was alert to techniques essential for survival in Soviet Russia. A young boy traveling alone could attract unwelcome attention, so I looked for a way to stay inconspicuous. Noticing a family with children, I hurried over to stand nearby so as to seem to belong with them. When the announcement came for the train to Tbilisi, I followed them into the same wagon and was with them on perhaps half my journey.

In every wagon there were seats below and two tiers of bunk beds above. I asked a non-Jewish passenger to help me put my baggage in the uppermost bunk bed where I thought I would be less conspicuous. As the train pulled out of the station, I started to feel calmer.

The road to Gruzia crosses the Caucasian mountains

Just as I was settling in comfortably, a new concern started to worry me: Where could I put on Tefilin to say my prayers the next morning? Once a fellow student of mine traveling by train had had an unfortunate experience: When he had put his Tefilin on to pray in a quiet corner, other passengers had raised an outcry at such a display of "religious incitement" and "propaganda" and he was lucky to escape unharmed.

After giving the problem much thought, I decided to put on my Tefilin very early, at daybreak, and read only the Shma prayer. Then I would climb down to floor level, hold my Siddur inside a newspaper, and say my prayers unnoticed by anyone.

The next morning I put on my Tefilin and started to read the Shma. Suddenly I was startled to see a non-Jewish passenger staring at me from the opposite bunk bed! Soon, I was convinced, he would tell everyone what I was doing. Rattling off the rest of the Shma as fast as possible, I pulled off my Tefilin, making sure to make no eye-contact with him so he could ask no questions.

Thankfully, he said nothing. But I realized that I dare not imperil myself a second time. So I was back to square one: How was I to put on Tefilin for the next two days?

After racking my brain for hours for a solution, I suddenly recalled the bottle of vodka and the carton of cigarettes Father had given me to take along. When I asked what they were for, he had replied: "You're traveling a long way and never know when they might come in good use." He was so right. Now the time had come.

Every wagon had its conductor, who had a little cabin for his personal use. Wrapping the vodka in a newspaper, I climbed down and knocked on the cabin door.

"What do you want?" shot back an angry voice with an accent, indicating that he was not Russian but belonged to one of the Soviet Union's many minority nationalities. I opened the door, holding out the vodka.

His eyes lit up. "Oh, what can I do for you?" he asked in a much more amiable tone...

"I am religious and need a quiet place to pray," I explained. "Could I use your room to pray tomorrow and the day after? It would take me about half an hour."

"Sure, go ahead! As far as I'm concerned, you can pray here all day!" he assured me as he eagerly took the vodka.

I climbed back to my bunk bed ecstatic with joy. The next morning I took my Tefilin to his cabin, and he left me there undisturbed. That prayer was a pure spiritual delight, permeated with undiluted joy. It was incredible that in those dark days, when observing the Torah's commandments was considered one of the worst crimes, I could don Tefilin on a train operated by the Soviet government with full permission of the conductor who even gave me his cabin for that purpose!

FEVER AND EXCRUCIATING PAIN

On the second or third day of my journey, I suddenly felt ill. My temperature shot up and I felt sharp pain at the base of my cheeks. Just trying to open my mouth was unbearably painful. Although I did not know what it was, I had caught the mumps.

Lying immobile on my bunk bed, I was consumed by excruciating pain with no way to alleviate it. A non-Jewish passenger noticed my suffering and offered to bring me a glass of hot water at the next stop. I thanked him and tried to drink it. But opening my mouth and attempting to swallow were so painful that I don't know if I even finished it.

The rest of my journey was one long bout of constant, unrelenting and excruciating pain. Still, I had already suffered so much during my short lifetime that by now suffering was nothing unusual for me...

Tbilisi, Gruzia: The train terminal

TBILISI

The train arrived in Tbilisi, capital of Gruzia, where I would have to wait until evening for the train to Kutais. What would I do till then? A boy

Tbilisi: A view of the city

sitting alone with a suitcase at the train station would arouse all sorts of suspicious questions. So I left my suitcase at the baggage office and went out for a walk, wrapping a towel around my throat because of my high fever.

Walking through the streets, I noticed a doctor's sign on a door. Perhaps he could help me. I knocked. He opened the door and I told him I had come on my own by train and was feeling ill. Taking my temperature, which was very high, he soon informed me that I had the mumps, which required bed rest for several days. If not treated properly, he warned, it could cause dangerous complications.

"How can I rest in bed?" I asked. "I'm in the middle of a long journey and still have to get to Kutais."

"I'm just telling you what you're supposed to do," he said. "Decide for yourself if you can follow my instructions."

Thanking him, I put on my coat and he helped me wrap the towel around my throat.

"Knowing the sickness is half the remedy," it is said. Now that I knew its name, I felt already half way to getting better...

The next few hours I spent wandering the city streets, sitting for a while in a park. At nightfall I went back to the station and retrieved my suitcase. When I got on my train, I again took the upper bunk bed.

ARRESTED AGAIN!

In the middle of the night, I awoke to the sound of loud knocking on the floor of my bunk bed. I opened my eyes to see the conductor, with a policeman next to him: "Get down! Together with your baggage..."

Finally they had caught up with me! After my escape to Homel, my journey to Moscow, then all the way south to Gruzia, they had traced me and caught me for escaping from the orphanage...

Terrified, I followed them to the conductor's cabin. They ordered me to open my suitcase. My Tefilin were the only suspicious articles I possessed, so I tried hiding them as best I could. But they were not interested in that. Examining my clothes, they noticed that all of them were new, and they exchanged meaningful glances.

"You're a speculator!" hissed the policeman.

I heaved a sigh of relief! At least I was not being arrested for escaping from the orphanage. As for "speculating" – illegal business – it was a charge I could easily disprove. (Later I learned that it was common practice for Gruzian Jewish businessmen to use boys to transport their merchandise illegally from one city to another.)

"Listen," I told them, "I'm not well and am traveling from Moscow to spend time at Tzchaltuba." That town was a renowned spa of natural hot baths where sick people from all over the Soviet Union came to get cured. "I don't know how long I'll have to stay there, so I've brought lots of new clothes with me. Take a look: they're all one size – my own size!"

The policeman did not understand Russian very well, but I managed to make myself understood and he realized I was telling the truth. With a high fever and looking worn after four days of travel, I certainly did not look like a typical "speculator."

"Okay," he told me. "Close your suitcase and go back to your place."

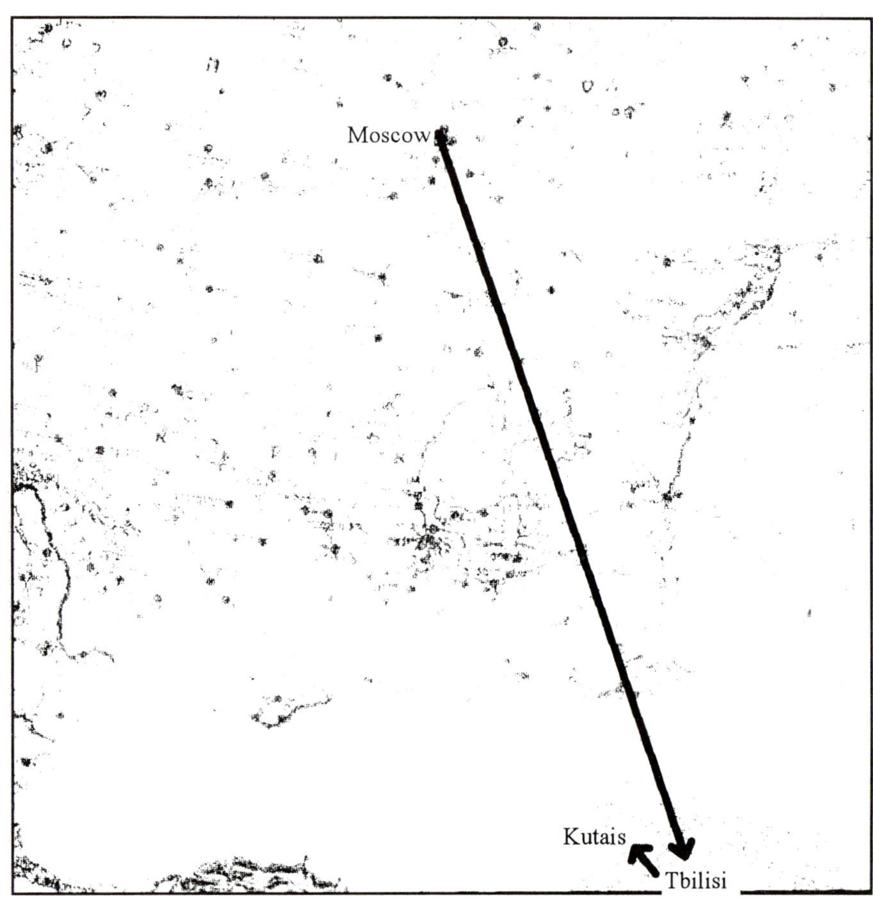

Four day journey to Tbilisi (Gruzia), getting ill with high fever

CHAPTER EIGHT

JEWISH LIFE IN GRUZIA

A NEW MEMBER OF THE FAMILY

The address I had been given in Kutais was the home of Reb Sender Menkin at 18 Macharazada Street. I asked the way and somehow managed to drag myself there with my last strength. But when I knocked at the door, it was opened by Gruzian Jews, who told me that the Menkins had moved to 35 Dmitrova Street.

Apparently, when their elderly mother had passed away, the Menkins had moved into her apartment.

I could hardly move. All I could think about was a bed in which to lay my aching body. Now I would have to walk even further.

Finally I arrived at the Menkins' home, drained of all strength and aching all over.

But the enthusiastic welcome they gave me was so utterly unexpected that it breathed fresh life into me. Although it was the first time they had ever set eyes on me,

Kutais: A view of the city

their welcome was so warm that an only child returning home after many years' absence could not have received a heartier one!

Reb Sender and his wife invited me to sit down, asking about my family and similar questions to make me feel at home. But soon I became very concerned, for I noticed that they had children, a son and two daughters, and the mumps is highly contagious.

"Do me one favor," I pleaded. "Please give me some corner of my own away from the family so that they shouldn't catch it."

But they refused to entertain the thought. "That is absolutely out of the question!" they declared. "Now that you're here, you're a member of our family. Whatever happens to you will happen to all of us. You've come to us, and you'll stay with us!"

It was an amazing way to treat a total stranger. For my part, I tried to stay in my corner, making every effort not to leave it except for dire necessity, so as not to infect their children.

A FAMILY OF CHARACTER

Reb Sender himself was a graduate of the original Tomchei Tmimim Yeshiva in the town of Lubavitch. A wonderful person with a heart of gold, he was a true Chossid with all his heart and soul. He served as Gabbai of the Lubavitcher Shul and earned his livelihood from weaving.

The whole family was extraordinarily generous and noble-hearted. His wife Eida (of the Lipsker family) was goodness personified, her every thought seeking to help others. In those days, there were no caterers and all weddings were prepared privately. For at least two days before any Jewish wedding in the city, Mrs. Menkin would be away from home all day and often all night, busy helping to prepare and organize everything for the wedding, with

Reb Sender and Mrs. Eida Menkin, with their daughters Zlata and Assia, after leaving the Soviet Union

boundless dedication.

After World War II, the Menkins settled in Paris. Many years later, when my son Yosef Yitzchok studied at Yeshivas Tomchei Tmimim at Brunoy, near Paris, he once wrote home asking how a Mrs. Eida Menkin was connected with our family. As soon as she had heard that my son was studying there, she sent him packages of sweets at every opportunity. That's what a good heart she had.

Their two daughters, too, Zlata and Assia, were similarly good-natured. Years later we learned that when food was scarce and rationed during World War II, they often gave up their own food and sent it to the Yeshiva so that we students would never go hungry and be able to study Torah in good health.

Reb Yehoshua Dubrawski

Eventually Zlata married Reb Refoel Wilschansky; settling in Paris. Unfortunately she passed away during childbirth in 1953, leaving three young sons. Assia is married to Reb Yehoshua Dubrawski, the renowned Yiddish writer, and they live in Crown Heights. The Menkins' outstanding son, Leib Henoch, will be described further on.

Mrs. Menkin's sister, Mrs. Menucha Lazarov (now living in Crown Heights), is also an exceptionally good-hearted person who lived with her husband Reb Leizer in Tbilisi. For several years after their marriage they had no children. Soon after she gave birth, with G-d's help, to their daughter Bat Sheva (now married to Rabbi Avrohom Shemtov, who heads Lubavitch in Philadelphia), Reb Leizer came to Kutais, where he danced in great joy. Later they had a son, Shimon (now married to the daughter of Reb Levi Yitzchok Schapiro of Crown Heights; they live in Houston, where he heads Lubavitch of Texas). During World War II, Reb Leizer was drafted into the Red Army and unfortunately never returned.

Reb Yaakov Lipsker and his wife Teibel

Living in Kutais were also Mrs. Menkin's brothers, Reb Leibel Lipsker (who lived later in Lud, Israel) and Reb Yaakov Lipsker (who lived later in Crown Heights), who then managed a government-owned textile factory. Financially he had his ups and downs, but the Yeshiva was always his first priority. His wife Teibel helped him in his charitable work, and their home was always open to everyone in need. Reb Leibel and his wife Malka also helped support the Yeshiva, as did their third brother, Reb Michoel Lipsker, when he lived in Kutais for a while (later, in 1950, he became our Rebbe's first Shaliach, in Meknes, Morocco, afterwards settling in Crown Heights in 1968).

The Lipskers' brother-in-law, Reb Moshe Neimark, who also lived in Kutais, was well-off, owning a workshop for manufacturing sweaters. He and his wife Luba were also great supporters of the Yeshiva. Later they lived in Montreal, Canada.

Another couple always very close and supportive of the Yeshiva was Reb Meir Shmukler and his wife Tzila, who lived in the same home as his parents. When World War II began, Meir was drafted into the Soviet Army and never returned. Tzila was left to support her two young sons, earning money by peddling clothing and also rye kernels, a popular grain in the Soviet Union which was cooked or ground into flour. She would carry fifty-kilo sacks of the grain on her shoulders to sell in Kutais and the surrounding villages. As often as she could, she invited students of the Yeshiva to her Shabbos table.

Later she married Rabbi Meir Chayim Chaikin (about whom we will write later), and afterwards Rabbi Yitzchok DovBer Ushpol, one of the Roshei Yeshiva of the Central Lubavitcher Yeshiva in Brooklyn, and the beloved Rabbi of a Lubavitcher Shul in Borough Park. Her two sons have raised fine families with many children and grandchildren.

THE AMAZING CURE

When I came to the Menkins, it was shortly before Pesach, 1938. It was very difficult to obtain Matza for Pesach, especially "Shmura" Matza (baked from flour guarded from becoming leavened since the grain was harvested). Every Chabad family, including the Menkins, had obtained just the minimum of Shmura Matza needed for their family, so my sudden arrival created a problem where to find Matzos for me. Obtaining ordinary Matza would have been easier, but I was particular to eat only Shmura Matza. In the end I asked each Chabad family to spare me just one or two Matzos till I had enough.

As I sat down to the Seder, I was still sick with the mumps.

Only with great pain could I open my mouth and chew the Matza, Moror (bitter herbs) and Korech (sandwich of Matza and Moror).

Present at the Seder were two of Mrs. Menkin's brothers, Mottel and Elya Lipsker, who were both still unmarried (Eliyahu later lived for many years in Toronto and some of his sons are important Shluchim of the Rebbe). After the main part of the Seder, when we were about to start the meal, the two young men suddenly announced that their Afikomen was missing and they were going to look for it. They signaled me to follow.

They went into a side room where they had hidden some pure, strong Gruzian kosher wine of excellent quality! (The wine we had used for the four cups was sweet and diluted and much cheaper in quality.) They poured out one cup after another for all three of us, wishing each other "L'chayim," till we had drank an extra four cups besides the four cups required at the Seder itself.

We returned to the table and started singing merrily. Before long we got up to dance, which we did more and more exuberantly, with joyous abandon. In my whole life I don't remember ever dancing with such intense joy as on that night.

It wasn't just the wine. Much more, it was a new-found sense of liberation and relief I had never before experienced. Till then my whole life had been spent under immense pressure. The continuous shadow of persecution, the constant fear of arrest and punishment, forced us to keep

Yiddishkeit secretly. Later I had to wander and flee from town to town, culminating in my recent ordeal in jail, followed by uncertainty about my future while at the orphanage, and fear of discovery after my escape. All this had cast a depressing pall of gloom over my life.

But in Gruzia I had finally reached a place where, incredibly, we were free to practice Yiddishkeit undisturbed. The resultant joy filling my heart overflowed on that night of Pesach – the "Time of Our Freedom" as we call it in our holiday prayers.

After drinking so much wine and dancing so merrily for so long, I went to sleep soaked in perspiration. The weather was already warm, too, for even winter is not really cold in Gruzia.

Next morning, I was amazed to wake up like a new person, my sickness fully cured. Yesterday I was aching all over and could hardly move, yet today all the pain was gone and I could barely remember my long ordeal!

Perhaps it was the heavy perspiration that cured me. But I like to think my cure came from fulfilling the commandment of eating Matza on the first night of Pesach, which the Zohar calls the "food of faith" and also, most relevantly for me then, the "food of healing."

INCREDIBLE FREEDOM

Compared with most of the Soviet Union, Gruzia's general atmosphere was one of incredible freedom. Just weeks before, when I had walked into the Shul in Moscow, a Lubavitcher, without even looking at me, had whispered to me to leave immediately for my own protection. But in

Gruzia, everything was different. It was like a dream, as if I had entered paradise or the Holy Land!

In Russia we had been afraid to have any contact with local Jews, both to avoid getting them into trouble and for fear of informers. But in Gruzia the local Jews openly showed great respect to Yeshiva students for being full-time students of the holy Torah.

Jews in Gruzia practiced Yiddishkeit freely and undisturbed. Besides three other Shuls located elsewhere in town, there were two large Shuls built close to each other which would be filled every Shabbos with 400 congregants each! On Friday night, when they all sang "L'choh Dodi" together, it was hard to believe this was happening in Stalin's Soviet Union! (It is said that this relative freedom was because Stalin himself was Georgian and deliberately left his fellow countrymen unhampered by the totalitarian stringency enforced throughout the rest of the Soviet Union.)

The Jews of Gruzia follow the customs of Oriental Jews (similar to those of the Sfardim), calling their Rabbis "Chacham." At that time they included Chacham Yaakov, Chacham Binyamin and several others.

Chacham Michael Davitashvili

The Rabbi at the above-mentioned great Shul was Chacham Michael Davitashvili, a unique personality and fiery speaker. One Shavuos I listened to his sermon, delivered in the Gruzian language. Although I did not understand a word, he spoke with such eloquence and enthusiasm, and his large audience listened with such rapt attention and silence, that I was spellbouned.

Rabbi Leivik Slavin

Chacham Michael was firm and authoritative. Once he discovered that a local Jewish butcher had sold non-kosher meat to a Jewish customer. Chacham Michael accosted the butcher and twisted his arm behind his back, forcing him to reveal the customer's name. He led him through the streets of the city to the customer's home, where he broke the earthenware utensils that had become non-kosher and he rekoshered the kitchen. Later I heard the Chacham telling how "he would have killed the butcher" if he hadn't told him the customer's name!

Despite the general freedom, the authorities sometimes did crack down. Unfortunately, Chacham Michael was arrested in 1941, on the same night as Rabbi Avrohom Levi (known as "Reb Leivik") Slavin, who had been sent to Gruzia in 1917 by the Rebbe RaShaB as his emissary to teach the local Jews. Both passed away in prison-camp, may G-d avenge their blood.

CHAPTER NINE

THE YESHIVA IN KUTAIS

BEGINNINGS

After Pesach, I turned fifteen and was eager to start studying in Yeshiva. But a Yeshiva did not yet exist. I was joined by another student, Mendel Raskin (son of Reb

Mendel Raskin together with the author after leaving the Soviet Union

Yaakov Yosef Raskin; both lived later in Kfar Chabad), who had also fled the persecution of the underground Yeshivos. Together with the Menkins' son Leib Henoch, we needed an advanced Torah teacher.

Rabbi Meir Chayim Chaikin, later Rosh Yeshiva in Montreal, Canada

In Kutais lived Rabbi Meir Chayim Chaikin (later Rosh Yeshiva of Yeshivas Tomchei Tmimim of Montreal, Canada; his sons are Rabbi Azriel Chaikin, now Rabbi of Brussels, Belgium, and Rabbi Sholom DovBer Chaikin, Rabbi of the Chabad community in Cleveland, Ohio). Rabbi Chaikin was a great scholar, permeated with Chassidic spirit, and a man of great personal sacrifice. He agreed to give us a daily lecture in the fifth chapter ("Eizehu Neshech") of Talmudic tractate Baba Metziya. I still remember his first lesson.

However, after teaching us for a while, Rabbi Chaikin informed us one day that he had to move to Tbilisi because he had no livelihood in Kutais. On a temporary basis, we were taught for a while by Reb Berel Kievman (son of the renowned Chossid Reb Dovid Horodoker; he lives now in Kfar Chabad).

A YESHIVA TAKES SHAPE

Meanwhile, the administrators of Tomchei Tmimim were starting to focus on Gruzia as an ideal location for undisturbed Torah study. They instructed Rabbi Yosef Goldberg – with whom I had stayed in Klintze - to go there to head the new Yeshiva.

Besides being an outstanding Torah scholar, erudite and profound, Reb Yosef was also devoted to every student with all his heart and soul, concerned not only with our educational progress but also with our material needs. Whenever we had no bread to eat, he would always rush out to find some, making sure that all our needs were satisfied.

After Reb Yosef arrived, it started to become a real Yeshiva. Many students soon joined our ranks, including Refoel Wilschanski, Heschel Tzeitlin, Velvel Averbach, Sholom Ber Pewzner, Leibel Motchkin, Azriel and Berel Schanowitz, Moshe and Sholom Marozov, Sholom Mendel

Rabbi Yosef Goldberg, serving later as Rosh Yeshiva in Brunoy, France

Our Yeshiva building in Kutais serves today as a storage outhouse for a synagogue

Kalmanson, Yaakov and Sholom Ber Notik ("Sholom-Ber Hagodol"), Chayim Osher Kahanov, Moshe Niselevitch and many others.

We studied diligently and enthusiastically, not wasting a moment. Gradually the constant fear we had experienced during our wanderings in Russia evaporated. We were happy to live among Jews, who treated us with the respect befitting students of the Torah.

After some time, Rabbi Yosef Goldberg became engaged to the daughter of Reb Michoel and Soroh – "Mumeh Sorke" – Katzenelenbogen. He had to leave to get married and establish a family.

LIVING WITH CHASSIDUS

It was then that the Almighty sent us a special gift, in the person of Rabbi Shmuel Notik ("Shmuel Krislaver"). This unique Chossid was overflowing with scholarship, both of "Nigleh" (the "revealed" part of the Torah – Talmud and Halacha) and Chassidus.

Day and night, Reb Shmuel lived with the letter and spirit of Chassidus. Often he would quote Reb Greinem (Rabbi Shmuel Greinem Estherman, the main Mashpiya – teacher of Chassidus – in the original Tomchei Tmimim in Lubavitch) who interpreted the prayer (Psalms 51:13) "Do not take from us Your holy spirit": Please do not deprive us of the little pleasure we get from studying Chassidus!

Reb Shmuel worked hard to imbue us with the true spirit of Chassidus, both in his lessons and in the Farbrengens he often held for us. I thank G-d for the great privilege of having studied under him. Any enthusiasm we have for Yiddishkeit and Chassidus is thanks to him.

Reb Shmuel would teach one group of students after another at various levels. He taught us the discourses of the Alter Rebbe's two classic works on the weekly Torah portions, "Torah Or" (on Bereishis, Shmos and Megilas Esther) and "Likkutei Torah" (on Vayikra, Bamidbar, Devorim and Shir Hashirim), besides mimeographed copies of the Rebbe RaShaB's discourses. He called on us to "live" all twenty-four hours of the day with the Maamar (discourse) we were studying, to pray with its inspiration, to think of it always, to "eat and sleep with it" – fulfilling its practical lessons even while eating and falling asleep.

Particularly memorable is the special atmosphere created when we studied the Maamar "L'chol tichloh..." of 5659 (1898). At that time we had only mimeographed copies of a manuscript. There (p. 112 in the published edition) the Rebbe RaShaB calls for serving G-d "by nullifying one's will, beyond one's nature and habituation, to transform one's heart from one extreme to the other, so that whatever the heart naturally is inclined to do, one should not do, and whatever the heart is inclined not to do, one should do."

For many weeks, we lived with this remarkable lesson for life. Day by day, Reb Shmuel continued to explain it with analogies and practical examples, engraving ever deeper into our minds and hearts the message that we should not do what we want, and should do what we don't want.

One year, during the High Holiday season, Reb Shmuel held a Farbrengen and spoke most inspiringly. Every Rosh Hashana, he told us, the Rebbe RaShaB would accept upon himself a new religious obligation or stringency in order to ensure that Rosh Hashana's inspiration would have a permanent effect upon his life.

Inspired by his words, I considered what extra obligation would be appropriate for me. I reminded myself that at my Bar Mitzva, Father had begged me to start wearing not only the usual Tefilin, which follow the Halachic ruling of RaShI, but also those following Rabbeinu Tam's ruling – as is the custom of Chassidim and others. At the time I had been unwilling to start wearing these additional Tefilin. It was not yet customary for young Bar Mitzva boys to wear them (until 1977, when our Rebbe introduced the present custom). I also was afraid to accept an obligation I was not sure I could keep under the difficult conditions of the time.

Now, however, I reconsidered. By starting to wear this second pair of Tefilin, I would be accepting a new obligation and also fulfilling the commandment of honoring my father. Father was still in Moscow, and I wrote to him about my decision. It was not long before he sent me a pair of Rabbeinu Tam's Tefilin!

SPECIAL STUDENTS

Reb Shmuel felt that two students, Refoel Wilschanski and Leib Henoch Menkin, were particularly well-suited for fully absorbing the teachings of Chassidus, and he devoted himself to their Chassidic education even more than to the rest of us.

Leib Henoch left an unforgetable impression on me. He absorbed all the Chassidic guidance that Reb Shmuel

The Great Synagogue in Kutais. At right are the two sons of the Shochet, Rabbi Eliyahu Chayim Panakishvili (a Chossid of the Rebbe RaShaB), who serve today as Chachamim in Kutais

poured into him, becoming the outstanding model of a true Chassidic student.

In his studies, both of Talmud and Chassidus, Leib Henoch was unusually diligent. But it was his prayer that was most special. Before starting morning prayers, Leib Henoch would follow our two-hour study of Chassidus with several hours of profound meditation on subjects of Chassidic philosophy. After that, his prayers on weekdays would take at least three to four hours of fervent worship, with extraordinarily sweet devotion. On Shabbos they would take much longer. Once I hid in his room to watch how he prepared for and recited his bedtime Shma prayers very slowly with deep devotion, which made a mighty impression on me.

Leib Henoch approached everything in life profoundly. For example, we students took turns every day picking up the food that was cooked for us elsewhere in town. Leib Henoch, however, although eager to do any other duty required of him, always tried to avoid leaving the Yeshiva environment of Torah study and service of G-d even for a short while. He would ask other students to take his turn, promising them some favor in return, such as writing out a Maamar for them (until our own generation, the vast Chabad Chassidic literature existed mostly in manuscript; to obtain a Maamar usually meant that it had to be written out laboriously in longhand).

Students of Leib Henoch's caliber were rare even then. But we learned to appreciate such special individuals who represent the true Chossid, who prepare for prayer by meditating on concepts of Chassidus about the greatness of G-d, then pray slowly word by word, feeling the meaning of every word with all their heart. After prayer, they spent the day with the constant thought of how to serve G-d better. They go to sleep only after a soul-searching accounting of their whole day, reciting the bedtime Shma with regret for anything unsatisfactory and a firm resolve that tomorrow will be better.

The present generation would gain much by learning to appreciate this classic portrait of a true Chossid and trying to emulate it, each according to his ability.

Although in Kutais we had wonderful conditions for growth in Torah and Chassidus, with an outstanding teacher and Mashpiya who was so devoted to him personally, Leib Henoch yearned for even more. Towards the end of my stay in Gruzia, Leib Henoch decided to leave for Samarkand, Central Asia, where he hoped to benefit from the special Chassidic guidance of the renowned Chossid and Mashpiya, Reb Nissan Nemanov, who headed a new branch of Tomchei Tmimim that had been established there during World War II.

REB SHMUEL'S SAYINGS

Some of Reb Shmuel's stories and sayings remain engraved on my mind and heart to this day. Here are a few examples:

A soldier on guard duty in the Czar's army one bitterly cold night felt that his feet were becoming frozen. Faithful to his duty, he stayed at his post without moving, although both his feet froze. Everyone was sure his extreme devotion would earn him a medal from the Czar. But the Czar ordered that he be given twenty-five lashes, because "his oath to serve his king faithfully should have warmed his whole body and prevented his feet from getting frozen!"

The Chossid from whom Reb Shmuel heard this told how the story had inspired him in his service of G-d for twenty-five years because, as our Sages tell us, all Jews took an oath at Mount Sinai to serve G-d with all our heart and soul, and this oath should warm us always...

After World War II, when I was in Fernwald, a DP (displaced persons) camp in Germany, I met some Gerer Chassidim and heard from one a story that reminded me of another of Reb Shmuel's sayings:

The Talmud (Avoda Zara 10b) tells of a notorious philanderer named Elozor ben Durdaya, who was provoked by a certain incident to realize how low he had sunk. Overwhelmed by the enormity of his sins, he wept and wept until his soul left him. At that moment, far off, the renowned Rabbi Yehuda Hanossi (compiler of the Mishna – basis of the Talmud – and respected and saintly leader of his generation), often known simply as "Rebbe," was teaching his disciples. Sensing what had happened to Elozor ben Durdaya, Rebbe suddenly started to weep, exclaiming: "A person is able to acquire 'his world' [reward in this world and the next] in one instant!"

Reb Shmuel asked: Why did Rebbe weep when he said this? On the contrary, he should have been happy that an individual has the opportunity to redeem his life in such a short time.

Reb Shmuel answered by explaining that each of us has his special auspicious moment which, if he loses it, he forfeits the purpose for which his soul came down into this world...

Here is the story I heard from the Gerer Chossid that illustrated for me Reb Shmuel's explanation:

When the second Gerer Rebbe, the saintly Rabbi Yehuda Leib Alter (author of "Sefas Emes"), passed away on 5 Shvat, 1905, it was an unusually bitter cold winter day. After the burial, it is customary for the mourners to walk shoeless between two rows of those who "comfort" them. The Chassidim begged the departed Rebbe's son and successor, Rabbi Avrohom Mordechai Alter (author of "Imrei Emes"), not to take off his shoes because the extreme cold of the snow-covered ground might harm his health. The new Rebbe was a renowned scholar in his own right, but he told them to ask a Rabbi who issues Halachic rulings. The Rabbi ruled that he must take off his shoes. One of the Chassidim present was so poor that he used to go begging for a living. When he saw the Rebbe starting to take off his shoes, he pulled off his own fur coat and threw it down on the ground in front of the Rebbe. Other Chassidim immediately followed his example, and the Rebbe walked shoeless over a path of fur coats! That year, the poor Chossid started doing so well financially that he became outstandingly wealthy. He had seized his special moment when it came and thus acquired "his world" in that one instant...

Some of Reb Shmuel's sayings penetrated so deeply into my heart that their effect lasts to this day. One memorable saying:

In our prayers we say: "They shall praise His Name with dance, with drum and harp they shall play to Him" (Psalms 149:3). Not everyone can play musical instruments, which require training and skill. Anyone, however, is capable of praising G-d by dancing, as long as he intends it sincerely with all his heart and soul.

This insight impressed me greatly. Ever since, whenever I attend a wedding, I try to liven it up with all my energy in order to make the bride and groom happy, which is a Torah obligation. After all, everyone is capable of "praising His Name with dance!"

Those seven years - 1938-1945 - that I spent in Kutais shaped my character for life.

CHAPTER TEN

LIVING WITH MIRACLES

THE DRAFT

Although religion was not persecuted in Gruzia as much as it was in Russia, there was no shortage of problems and dangers.

In the summer of 1941, Germany invaded the Soviet Union, which then began a desperate struggle for its very survival. Throughout the land, every male over 18 was drafted into the Red Army. Even those previously granted exemption had to report again, and exemptions were granted only to those who were really sick. Tens of millions of Soviet soldiers died in the war, and the likelihood of returning from the front was minimal.

Under such circumstances, we Yeshiva students learned to live with continuous miracles. Although we were all healthy young men of draft age, not one of us was actually drafted! Whoever did not live through that stormy period cannot appreciate what an astounding miracle that was. G-d watched over us all, as the Mishna says (Avos 3:5): "Whoever accepts upon himself the yoke of Torah has the yoke of governmental and worldly obligations removed from him."

Each of us saw his own personal miracles during that time. Here are a few that stand out in my memory:

"CONTINUE ON YOUR WAY!"

The government required everyone to be registered in his place of residence and report there to the draft office upon reaching military age. Even after receiving an exemption, one had to report back every year to have it extended.

Among the students was Reb Shmuel Notik's son Yaakov (he lives now in Nachalas Har Chabad, Kiryat Malachi, Israel). Yankel was registered in Kutais. When draft summonses started reaching his address, he simply ignored them. That meant he had no valid identification documents, which was very dangerous, for the police often made house-to-house searches, demanding every adult male's identification documents and proof of exemption. Anyone unable to provide them was hauled off to the police

Reb Yaakov Notik, in recent years

station and usually sent straight to the front.

Not far from Kutais, in the spa-town of Tzchaltuba, someone managed to obtain from the draft office a quantity of "white cards" – indicating full exemption from military service. They were half stamped with the official stamp, the other half being added onto the picture of whoever bought such an illicit card for a high price. Although these cards would not be accepted by the local draft office, which could check its own records of anyone's true status, they were enough to satisfy a policeman asking for documents.

Yankel traveled to Tzchaltuba and bought one of these white cards, to have it ready in case of need.

The director of the Kutais draft office was a non-Jew named Meskhe who recognized us all, knowing exactly which of us had reported to the draft and which not.

Once Yankel had a fright. He saw Meskhe in the street and realized he had noticed him. Meskhe was well aware that Yankel had avoided the draft and would surely arrest him. The game was over, and Yankel expected the worst.

"Hey, Notik, have you been to Tzchaltuba?" called out Meskhe.

"Yes," replied Yankel, who saw no point in denying it.

"Continue on your way!" Meskhe told him.

Yankel returned to the Yeshiva still shaking with shock from his close escape. Instead of arresting him on the spot, Meskhe had demonstrated that he was fully aware of the various ruses for avoiding the draft, and yet had told him "Continue on your way!" It was nothing short of miraculous...

CAUGHT TWICE AND SAVED

Moshe Niselevitch (now living in Nachalas Har Chabad and director of "Chamah," which aids Russian-speaking Jews in Israel, the USA and the ex-Soviet lands) also experienced an amazing miracle.

Reb Moshe Niselevitch, in recent years

His father, Reb Chayim, was a scholar who studied Torah full time, leaving Moshe to support the family. Moshe would spend all day at the Yeshiva until late in the evening, then go to work for several hours on the night shift at Reb Moshe Neimark's sweater workshop to earn money for the family.

Moshe, too, had ignored his draft summonses. Once, while walking at night to or from work in the non-Jewish neighborhood of Byele Must ("White Bridge"), the police stopped him. With no valid documentation, he was arrested and taken to the draft office.

There Meskhe yelled at him indignantly: "You counter-revolutionary, enemy of the Soviet government! It is your civic duty to be drafted into the army and help the national war effort!"

After venting his anger he told him: "Go home, pack up,

and say goodbye to your parents. Report back here tomorrow morning."

After such a heated outburst, Moshe was amazed to be released. Taking it as a sign that Meskhe was not serious, he did not report back. He continued his daytime schedule of Yeshiva study and work at night, trying to avoid the police on his way there and back.

However, he was caught again. This time Meskhe was seething.

Pressing his revolver against Moshe's head, he declared: "I have pity on you only because I know your parents. Go home and return immediately to be drafted. If you don't turn up, I myself will shoot you in the head!"

Moshe promised to return. This second release was an even greater miracle, for Meskhe could have sent him immediately to the front; Moshe had already proved himself unreliable, disobeying a previous order to return, so how could Meskhe rely on him?

Moshe came into the Yeshiva to bid us farewell. After he told us what had happened, he said goodbye and turned to leave. But Moshe Marozov, the eldest student among us, barred his way: "You're not leaving!" he said firmly.

"What do you mean? He'll kill me otherwise!"

"And if you get sent to the battlefront, won't you get killed?" retorted Morozov.

Someone had an idea. Reb Dovid Perlow (son of Rabbi Mordechai Perlow, who had been sent by the Previous Rebbe to serve as Rabbi to the Jews of Gruzia – both moved later to Melbourne, Australia) had an electric shaver. One of the students ran to bring it to Marozov, who announced: "I hereby fulfill the Torah commandment that 'You shall be very careful to preserve your lives.' According to that commandment, there is no doubt that the Almighty wants you at this moment to shave off your beard!"

Grabbing hold of Moshe, he shaved off his beard. Now Meskhe would never recognize him! That is how he was able to remain inconspicuous so that he could stay in Kutais, avoiding near-certain death at the battlefront.

JUMP FROM A MOVING TRAIN

I once traveled with Moshe Marozov to Kulashi. On our way back we had a miracle of our own.

Our train had just one more stop before Kutais at a town called Riyon, when we were accosted by a policeman. His red cap and uniform indicated that he was a member of the Soviet police, who were much stricter than the local Gruzian officers. He ordered us to report to him when the train reached Riyon, as he wanted to speak to us. But he did not bother watching us until then as it was impossible to escape on the train.

Moshe told me to follow him. We went from car to car till we came to the back door of the last one. "Are you ready to jump out while the train is moving?" he asked.

"If you jump," I replied cautiously, "so will I!"

Moshe must have had previous experience doing this. It had to be done from the last car, he explained, because jumping from any other could sweep one under the train wheels from the rush of air. He instructed me how to jump safely as the train slowed down as it approached its stop.

Moshe set the example. Soon after the train began to slow down, he jumped out, turning over several times as he hit the ground. Amazingly, he stood up unharmed!

Now it was my turn! Silently I prayed to G-d, as Father had taught me: Please let me come out of this unharmed, without injury to any of my limbs. But if I am destined to die, I prayed, at least let me be privileged to have a Jewish burial.

I jumped! As I landed, I turned over a few times as Moshe had taught me. Thank G-d, I got up on my feet unharmed, as the train disappeared into the distance...

Opposite the rails was a steep slope, on top of which we could see cars driving on a highway. We climbed up and hitched a ride with a truck back to Kutais, safe from the Soviet police...

IN THE LION'S JAWS!

In 1942 I experienced an incredible miracle. To this day, whenever I recall the danger I was in, a chill runs down my spine.

Before Pesach, we needed a large new sieve to sift the flour for Matzos, and I was sent to another city to buy it. Arriving back in Kutais, I was shocked to see the train station swarming with police and soldiers. They had blocked one end of the platform, directing all alighting passengers to the other end where the police carefully inspected everyone's documents. If satisfied, they let the bearer leave. But the slightest suspicion was enough for them to order him to stand to the side, where other police officers would investigate him more thoroughly.

As noted, Father had originally registered me in the official records as three years younger than my true age, so that my year of birth was 1926. When the time came for those born that year to report for the draft, I managed to obtain new documents recording my year of birth as 1928, thereby gaining two more years.

That was fine on paper. But when I actually had to show a policeman my documents, according to which I was over four years younger than my real age, it was impossible to hide the truth. My papers showed that I was still fourteen, when I was really over nineteen! Any policeman inspecting my documents would take one look at me and realize that they had been falsified, invalidating them.

Like a cornered animal, I wandered around the station seeking some avenue of escape. But there was none. There was no choice but to fall into their hands...

I waited in line until it was my turn to present my documents.

"Where's your draft exemption card?" asked the policeman.

"I don't need one yet," I replied.

He burst out laughing. Without even glancing at my official age, he gave my papers to the policeman standing next to him, sending me to the left side where the other suspects were lined up for investigation. Now I was caught in the lions' den with nowhere to flee...

Just then, however, occurred a miracle which, if I had not

experienced it myself, I would never have believed possible.

Two Kutais Jews already drafted into the army were returning home for a furlough, still wearing their army uniforms. They were standing in the line right next to me. Realizing the danger I was in, they stood between me and the policeman who escorted me. In that moment, when I was concealed from his sight, I was able to merge with those already permitted to leave, and I escaped!

I hurried out of the station. But the police still had my documents, which included the address of my sleeping accommodations. Obviously I could not return there, because they would come to look for me.

Close to the train station lived the Menkins, and I ran there as fast as I could. Eida Menkin opened the door and was shocked to see me in a state of fright obvious on my face.

"Chatzkel, whatever happened?"

When I told her how I had fled from the police, she hid me until the evening. After dark, I went to the home of Reb Dovid Perlow, who concealed me in his sweater workshop in the basement.

My documents listed my address as a house owned by a Jewish woman whose family name was Eligulashvili. In the middle of the night the secret police came knocking at her door, showing her my picture and asking if I lived there. Yes, she replied, but I had gone away somewhere, she did not know where.

For two weeks the secret police watched that house and the Shul in the hope of spotting me. But I remained in hiding. However, hiding in Perlow's basement was only a temporary solution. Without documentation, I could not walk out of the house.

Not far from Kutais was the town of Zugdidi, a commercial center where many Kutais Jews traveled for business. A Jew who lived there, Mr. Reuven Tabdidishvili, had excellent contacts with key government officials in the town, including some in the local secret police. When asked to try to arrange documents for me, he suggested that I come to Zugdidi.

The problem was how to get there safely. Just going outside was dangerous for me, and traveling by train much more so. Even riding by car was a problem, for during wartime the police often set up road blocks to inspect people's documents.

After thoroughly considering all alternatives, it was decided that I go to Zugdidi by train, from the same station where I had been caught! Leib Henoch Menkin accompanied me, buying both our tickets while I waited outside. Only when we heard the whistle for the train to leave did we run into the station, catching the train after it had already started to move. Thus we were able to avoid all inspections, and arrived in Zugdidi safely.

After I met with Reuven Tabdidishvili, he spent a few days considering his options. For the past several days the police had been arresting all men without documents, many of them vagrants, taking them to the draft office for medical check-ups to determine whether they could be drafted. Reuven decided that I should join that group, while he marshaled his contacts to get me an official exemption card.

One of Reuven's highly placed secret-police contacts asked to see me before he would intervene on my behalf. He took one look at me and told me to go. Later he told Reuven that he could not intervene for me directly. He promised not to work against me or have me arrested, but suggested that Reuven enlist the aid of lower officials.

My medical tests were scheduled for Shabbos at midday. That morning, in the local Shul, Chacham Yitzchak Michaelshvili stood up and announced that the Yeshiva student Yechezkel Brod was to appear that day at the draft office and needed Divine mercy. He asked everyone to come to the draft office in case I needed help, as it involved the important Halachic duty of Pidyon Shvuyim – liberating those taken captive by non-Jews.

Reuven had expected I would be checked by a doctor he knew, who would grant me full exemption. Unfortunately, the doctor was absent that day and I was examined by a different one. Affected by the whole situation and weakened from weeks of hiding in the basement, I did not look well. The doctor looked me over and wrote: "Not fit for combat." That meant that although I would not be sent to the battlefront, I could still be drafted for non-combatant duties.

Chacham Yitzchak, who accompanied me, quickly alarmed his congregants who were waiting in the next room. They brought me in to them and, when they noticed the police not paying attention, spirited me outside.

I returned to the Shul with mixed feelings. On the one hand, I had eluded being drafted, but on the other hand my movements were still limited by having no official documents.

Meanwhile, I had a surprise visit. During my absence, my sister Reizel had married Reb Zalman Leib Estulin. Later he had been drafted into the Red Army and was wounded in action, resulting in his release. Now he was on his way to rejoin his family who now lived in Tashkent. Hoping to meet me, he arranged to travel through Gruzia and managed to track me down in Zugdidi.

Our meeting was deeply emotional. He was the first member of my family I had seen in over four years, and my situation was desperate. When it was time for him to leave, I burst into uncontrollable tears like a young child. All my pain and distress came out in those heartfelt tears. Even today Zalman Leib reminds me of it; he never would have imagined, he says, that I would cry so emotionally.

Eventually, documents were arranged for me somehow and I was able to return to Kutais to lead a more normal existence. At the first opportunity after my return that the Torah was read publicly, I recited the "HaGomel" blessing, as the Halacha requires, to thank G-d for my release from danger.

One of the congregants told me: "Chatzkel, you have not acted correctly! You've said the HaGomel blessing for just one incident when you should be saying it every day for all the miracles G-d does for you constantly!"

In truth, he expressed our situation exactly, for everything related here is but a tiny fraction of our miraculous experiences during the wartime years.

CHAPTER ELEVEN

AFTER THE WAR

LIVING REGARDS

When I arrived in Gruzia in 1938, I was a young boy just turning fifteen. Over seven years later, when the war ended in 1945, I was a grown man of twenty-two. As the excitement of war and then victory calmed down, I decided to take the opportunity to visit my parents who had escaped to Tashkent in 1941 after the German invasion.

World War II: A snow-covered battlefield near Moscow

At the victory march in Moscow at the end of World War II, the Nazi flag is lowered to the ground

My documents were still not completely in order, but I took the risk of making the long journey, first by train to the Caspian Sea, then by ship to Kislovod, then again by train to Tashkent in Uzbekistan, Central Asia.

Although I did not have my parents' address in Tashkent, I had the address of the Shul. Sure enough, when I arrived, there was Father standing ready like Avrohom our ancestor to greet wayfarers!

He did not recognize me. When he had last seen me seven years earlier, I had been a short, skinny boy. Now I had grown and broadened, and my face was covered by a bushy black beard that had barely started to sprout last time he had seen me.

Tashkent: The central square

Seeing a young stranger carrying a heavy suitcase, he was at my side instantly – so fast that it seemed as if he had jumped out of a window! Father's amazing kindness for even a total stranger was revealed once again!

After taking my suitcase, he gave me his hand to wish me "Sholom Aleichem!" I waited to see if he would recognize me.

"From where have you traveled?" he asked.

"From Kutais," I replied.

"Oh, from Kutais!" Father started to get excited. "I have a son living there. Maybe you have regards from him?"

I could restrain myself no longer: "Your regards are standing right here in front of you!"

Father looked at me. Although I had changed so much during those seven years, he managed to recognize my features behind my beard. He burst into tears of deep emotion and joy, and began reciting all possible blessings specified by the Halacha for such joyous moments: "Boruch... Shehecheyonu...," "Boruch... HaTov V'Hameitiv," "Boruch... M'Chayeh Ha'Meisim."

He brought me into the Shul and someone hurried to tell Mother of my arrival. When she saw me from afar, she fainted...

REUNION WITH THE FAMILY

For two weeks I rested from the long journey, taking the opportunity to reacquaint myself with the members of my family. They could barely recognize me. My younger brother Yisroel was a total stranger to me, having been just a year old the last time I saw him. My sister Soroh, too, had been a young girl when I had left and now became very attached to me.

My parents urged me to settle down. My life had been hard enough till then, they felt, suggesting that I find a job or learn a trade, and perhaps seek a suitable match. I was offered several positions teaching Torah to younger students.

But I refused to hear of it. How could I possibly leave

My parents with my sister Soroh and brother Yisroel, after the war

Tomchei Tmimim? I planned to continue at the Yeshiva's branch in Samarkand, which was not far from Tashkent. However, Reb Nissan Nemanov, head of the Yeshiva there, was unwilling to accept me, as the Yeshiva was already full and he felt that I had studied in Yeshiva long enough. Only thanks to the intervention of the renowned Chossid Reb Mendel Futerfas was I finally accepted.

My farewell from my parents was deeply emotional. We had no idea when, if ever, we would meet again. Mother seemed to have a premonition when she declared: "I don't even know if I will be at your wedding!" Indeed, she was right. I did not meet my parents again for many years.

SAMARKAND

My first question on arriving in Samarkand was: "Where is Leib Henoch Menkin?" Every student I asked avoided giving me a straight answer. I began to realize that something had happened. Finally someone revealed that Leib Henoch was no longer alive. He had caught malaria the summer he arrived and had passed away.

My world fell in. I had been so attached to him, with all my heart, for he had been such a rare person. I begged one of the students, offering him any money he wanted, to take me to Leib Henoch's grave.

Our Sages say that "No one can transcribe the feelings of the heart." I have no words to describe the terrible pain I felt to be unable to ever enjoy his company again...

THE CHANGING SITUATION

Meanwhile, the situation in the Soviet Union was changing. During the war, the secret police had tended to divert their attention from such "crimes" as religious observance in order to concentrate on wartime concerns such as draft-dodging and counter-espionage.

Another reason for the lull in religious persecution during the war was the influx of Polish Jews. In 1939, the Soviet Union had annexed the eastern part of Poland, with its million or so Jews. Especially after the Germans invaded the Soviet Union in 1941, thousands of Polish Jews escaped by fleeing deep into the USSR, many taking refuge in Central Asia, particularly in Tashkent and Samarkand. Recognizing their difference from its own citizens, the Soviet police had not hounded them excessively for religious activities.

Meanwhile, the Lubavitcher Chassidim, too, benefited from their presence. During the war, Cheder schools, Yeshivos, prayer gatherings in private homes and Mikvaos were able to operate largely undisturbed, because they were attributed to the Polish Jews. Individual Lubavitchers, too, often found it convenient to give the impression that they were Polish.

Now, however, the Polish Jews were leaving. As the Red Army advanced across Eastern Europe, it installed in all lands it occupied governments that were sympathetic to the Soviet Union, ensuring that all Eastern European states became its satellites. As a gesture of goodwill to Poland's new Communist government, the Soviets now permitted all

Polish refugees to return to Poland.

This exodus of Polish Jews worried the Lubavitchers. No longer could they find shelter under the pretext of being Polish. Already there were signs of a renewed cracking down on religious observance. Although Tomchei Tmimim had flourished relatively undisturbed during the war, the leading Chassidim began considering a new place of refuge for the Yeshiva in the future.

BACK TO GRUZIA

Reb Mendel Futerfas in his later years

After I had spent several months in Samarkand, Reb Nissan asked me to return to Gruzia to explore the possibility of moving Tomchei Tmimim there. "The Yeshiva won't be able to stay here much longer," he said. "But in Gruzia it has a chance of survival." Since I had spent seven years there and was familiar with the country, he asked me to go there and rent suitable buildings to prepare a future place of refuge.

Under the conditions of those days, my personal wishes were utterly irrelevant. Although I was not keen on going, the mission was necessary and I had been selected to do it, so nothing else was important...

Once more I set out for Gruzia, accompanied by Moshe Levertov (now in Crown Heights). He had 30,000 rubles on him for the requirements of our mission, especially for renting the buildings needed.

When our train reached Riyon, the station before Kutais, a policeman accosted us and asked us to follow him. We were terrified that he would discover the money and decide to investigate the source of such a large sum of cash, the possession of which was a cardinal crime in the Soviet Union.

As we passed a news-stand owned by a Gruzian Jew, I implored him to help us. He obliged, inviting the policeman inside his booth. A few minutes later, the policeman emerged and walked off. The owner asked us to reimburse him for the sixty rubles he had laid out: "That's how much it cost me to take care of you!"

THE GREAT DEBATE

We started to implement Reb Nissan's plan. Then we heard of a daring new plan some Lubavitchers had devised for leaving the Soviet Union by using false Polish passports.

Actually, there was a fierce debate about whether to take this dangerous step. Attempting to leave the country illegally was one of the Soviet Union's worst crimes, punishable even by death, and many questioned whether Jewish law permitted exposing oneself to such a risk. Others questioned whether it was morally permissible for Lubavitchers, who had been the activists responsible for preserving the flame of Judaism in the Soviet Union, to abandon the land's other Jews – including many other Lubavitchers and Torah-observant Jews unable to leave – to the mercies of the oppressive regime.

On the other hand, many argued that since conditions were likely to worsen again, every risk was worthwhile in order to leave the Soviet hell for other lands, where they would be free to raise their children as Torah-observant Jews.

An attempt was made to ask the advice of the Rebbe, Rabbi Yosef Yitzchok, who had reached Brooklyn, New York, in 1940. A telegram, phrased cryptically to conceal its true meaning from the Soviets, was sent to someone who could ask the Rebbe personally. However, it was impossible at that distance to explain all the details involved, which anyway were changing constantly, and the reply was therefore inconclusive. Some felt that the Rebbe's reply did leave room for proceeding with the plan, while others felt they could not leave without the Rebbe's explicit approval.

We received a letter from Reb Nissan telling us he was taking no stand in this debate, and giving us permission to leave Gruzia if we choose to join those seeking to escape.

PREPARING TO ESCAPE

Rabbi Mordechai ("Mottel") Perlow and his son Reb Dovid decided to join the group seeking to escape. I accompanied them on their journey from Kutais to Lemberg (Lvov), in Ukraine near the Polish border, from where the special trains (known as "echalons" – French for train cars) for Polish expatriates were leaving for Poland. In order to conceal my beard, I carried Reb Dovid Perlow's young son Zalman in my arms wherever we went.

In Lemberg, a Beth Din (Halachic law court) of prominent Lubavitcher Rabbis reviewed the question from the standpoint of Jewish law and ruled that those willing to take the risk were permitted to do so. A group of leading activists organized the escape down to the last detail, including expert changes to many hundreds of Polish passports bought for hefty sums from returning Jewish refugees whose relatives had passed away during their years of hunger and suffering in the Soviet Union.

Sometimes, when passport names indicated a husband and wife, unmarried couples had to pretend to be husband and wife. For example, for passport purposes, I was considered to be married to the sister-in-law of the Shochet Reb Yisroel Shimon Kalmenson (her husband, Reb Shmuel Marozov, had been arrested in 1938 and beaten to death in front of his father, Reb Elchonon Dov – "Chonye" – Marozov, although she did not find it out until two decades later).

We received these false passports with our new names right before getting onto the train. The terrible fear that gripped us all made me anxious about forgetting my new identity written in the unfamiliar Latin alphabet on the passport.

In each wagon, the Soviet police set up a table and asked all travelers to pass by one by one when our names were called. I asked Rabbi Mottel Perlow to pinch me when they called out my new name. Thank G-d, everything proceeded without incident.

As our train pulled out of the station, Reb Yisroel Neveler stood up on one of the seats and read out Tefilas Haderech, the prayer said when traveling. Tearfully, each of us repeated the words after him, asking G-d to bless our trip: "...Lead us safely, direct our steps safely, guide us safely...and bring us to our destination alive, happily and safely. Save us from the hands of every enemy, lurking foe, robber and wild animals on the way, and from all kinds of calamities that may come to afflict the world. Bestow blessing upon all our actions, and grant me favor, kindness and mercy in Your eyes and in the eyes of all who see us...and hear the voice of our prayer..."

Reb Yisroel Neveler (Levin), after leaving the Soviet Union

During those dramatic moments, when each of us felt our lives at stake, tears flowed like water from the eyes of every man, woman and child crowded into our wagon. Years later, at such high points of spiritual arousal as Ne'ila, the concluding prayer of the fast of Yom Kippur, holiest day of the Jewish year, I can only hope to achieve such a heartfelt spiritual arousal as we experienced in those fearful moments.

Once again, as I had learned from Father, I appealed to G-d, using my name and my mother's name, to beg Him that I and everyone else there escape safely. Thank G-d, we crossed the border to Poland uneventfully, leaving the hated land of Russia behind us.

Looking back, the entire escape was an amazing miracle: Our train was packed with "Polish" citizens, not one of whom was actually Polish! Nevertheless, in this way many hundreds of Lubavitcher Chassidim succeeded in escaping safely to the free world.

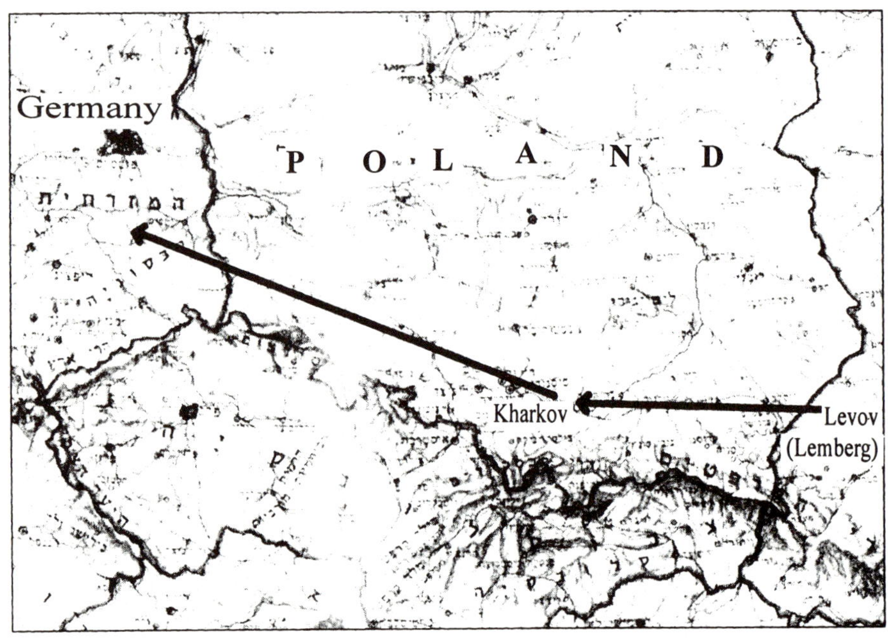

From Levov (Lemberg) we crossed the border to Poland, and headed to Germany

CHAPTER TWELVE

LIFE AS REFUGEES

POLISH ANTI-SEMITISM

We had left the hated Soviet Union. But we were not yet out of trouble. Soviet troops still occupied all of Eastern Europe.

After we arrived in Poland, we were assisted by the renowned "Bricha" ("escape") activists, whose goal was to help Jews travel to the Holy Land, then still under the British mandate. With great courage they worked to get Jews out of Eastern Europe, which held such tragic memories of the Holocaust years. With these lands now occupied by the Soviets, who were not happy with the idea of people emigrating to the free world, the Bricha had to spirit Jews out of Eastern Europe by clandestine means.

There was another reason for the Bricha wanting to speed our passage through Poland. It was literally dangerous for Jews to stay there because of the Poles' virulent anti-Semitism. Of Poland's three and a half million Jews in

1939, over three million had perished in the war, most of them murdered by the Germans – with the approval and active participation of their willing accomplices, the Poles. When emaciated concentration camp survivors returned after the war to reclaim their homes and possessions, many were brutally murdered by their old Polish neighbors. There were even pogroms, such as at Kielce, where Poles murdered scores of Jews. Even travel by train was dangerous for Jews, for the Poles would often throw them off moving trains.

We had to be extra careful not to give away our Soviet origin, for Soviet troops were everywhere and it could have cost us our lives. The Bricha warned us not to speak to police or officials even in Yiddish, for our Yiddish dialect was full of Russian words that could identify us as Soviet nationals. Instead, we were told to answer questions with words from "Y'kum purkon" (a prayer in the Aramaic language said on Shabbos) and the like, or at least in Hebrew. Many did not remember Aramaic prayers by heart and their Hebrew grammar was so weak that their efforts to speak Hebrew were hilarious. Often those who heard their attempts at speaking Hebrew found it hard not to burst out laughing!

We spent just one Shabbos in Poland, in the city of Cracow. A group of us went to Shul for Mincha and got a bitter taste of Polish anti-Semitism. As we passed a group of wagon-drivers, they started towards us, snapping their whips with such a fierce look of brute hatred in their eyes that, if we hadn't managed to escape, they would surely have killed us. After Shabbos, seeing how dangerous it was to stay in Poland, we hurried to leave the country.

ENGAGEMENT AT POKING

We passed through Vienna and several other cities until we succeeded in entering the American-occupied zone of Germany, where we settled in the "displaced persons (DP) camp" at Poking. A number of Lubavitcher Chassidim were already there, including Reb Nissan Nemanov, who soon organized a branch of Tomchei Tmimim with scores of students. Besides being a place of refuge, Poking became a flourishing Torah center.

While I was at Poking, three weddings were held: Reb Sholom Ber Laine's, Reb Mottel Levin's (he was Reb Yisroel Neveler's son), and my own. I became engaged to my wife Teibel in 1947. The person who suggested the match was Reb Yisroel Meir Munitz (who himself had met his wife at the suggestion of my sister Tzivia and her husband, Reb Yaakov Galinsky, who had also left the Soviet Union). Years later, after both we and the Munitz family settled in Crown Heights, we became related by marriage when my son Sholom Ber married Reb Yisroel Meir's daughter Chana.

MY WIFE'S FAMILY

Teibel's father, Reb Yitzchok Dovid Gorchover, had studied in the original Tomchei Tmimim in Lubavitch, where he was known as "Dovid Babrinitzer." Later he lived in Krementchug, Ukraine, where Teibel was born. He was

My father-in-law,
Reb Yitzchok Dovid Gorchover

My mother-in-law,
Mrs. Chava Gorchover

employed as a bookkeeper, but secretly practiced as a Shochet (ritual slaughterer) and Mohel (circumcisor). His wife, Teibel's mother, was called Chava (nee Silberman).

During the war, her father had found refuge in the town of Bisk, Siberia, where he established a Shul and built a Mikvah. In secret he would slaughter chickens for anyone who requested it. My wife told me that once the secret police had come to arrest him, bringing a dog to sniff out his slaughter-place in a woodshed. He remained in the shed, leaning against the wood blocks to hide. Although his slaughtering knife was still dripping with blood, the dog did not smell it or discover his hiding place, thank G-d.

My father-in-law lost three of his sons during or right after the war: Berel, Moshe (killed in Poland after the war) and Avrohom Abba. His oldest son, Shneur Zalman, later emigrated to New York and lived here until he passed away. Another daughter, Dina, whose married name is Gurary, lives in Brooklyn, and a third daughter, Golda, whose married name is Goldovsky, lives in Kiryat Malachi, Israel.

Several years later, after we arrived in the United States, I found out more about my father-in-law from an unexpected source: Once when we spent a Shabbos on the Lower East Side of Manhattan, someone came and presented us with some beer in our honor. It was Rabbi Yaakov Leizer, who now serves as a Rebbe in Antwerp,

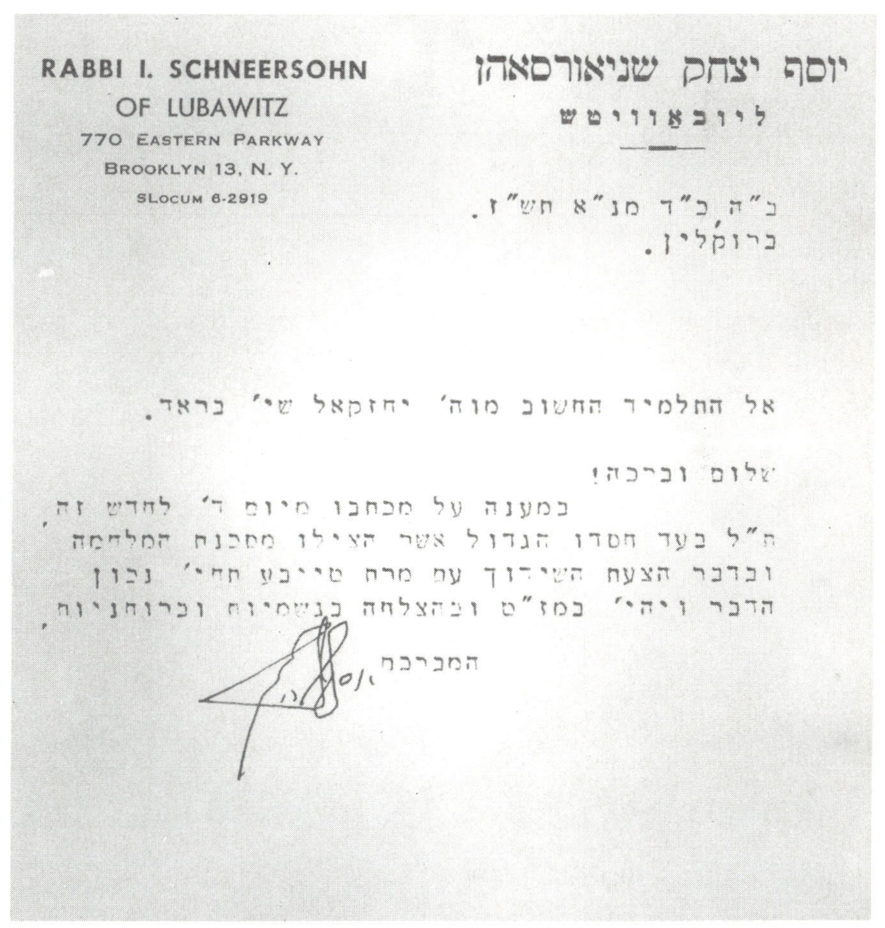

RABBI I. SCHNEERSOHN
OF LUBAWITZ
770 EASTERN PARKWAY
BROOKLYN 13, N. Y.
SLOCUM 6-2919

יוסף יצחק שניאורסאהן
ליובאוויטש

ב"ה, כ"ד מנ"א תש"ז.
ברוקלין.

אל התלמיד החשוב מוה' יחזקאל שי' בראד.

שלום וברכה!

במענה על מכתבו מיום ד' לחדש זה, ת"ל בעד חסדו הגדול אשר הצילו מסכנת המלחמה, ובדבר הצעת השידוך עם מרת טייבע תחי' נכון הדבר ויהי' במז"ט ובהצלחה בגשמיות וברוחניות,

המברכו

The Rebbe's letter, dated 24 Menachem Av, 5707 (1947), blessing our marriage

Belgium, succeeding his famous father-in-law, Rabbi Yitzchok Psheversker, who was a Rebbe in Paris and later in Antwerp.

After Shabbos, Reb Yaakov Leizer told us why he had brought the beer. During the war, he too had found refuge in Bisk, but was penniless. My father-in-law had noticed that his shoes were torn and had bought him brand new boots. When his own children found out about it, they complained bitterly that he had bought boots for a total stranger when they themselves needed new shoes. He explained to them: "You have a home, thank G-d. If anything happens to you, someone is here to take care of you. He, however, is a stranger here on his own, and if anything happens to him, G-d forbid, who will take care of him?"

Reb Yaakov Leizer was deeply moved by this act of charity for a stranger, and felt he had to show his appreciation even in a some small way.

My brother-in-law Reb Yaakov Galinsky, and my sister Mrs. Tzivia Galinsky, with some of their family

THE WEDDING

Mother's premonition came true. My parents were

not present at my wedding. My only relatives there were my sister Tzivia and her husband Reb Yaakov Galinsky.

The wedding took place not long after our engagement. The Menkins, too, had arrived in Poking, and once again it was Eida Menkin who, with her spectacular warmth and generosity of heart, took care of the whole affair, devoting herself to its preparation with all her energy. She worked for several days and nights, not even returning home for days at a time, to ensure that everything was prepared as nicely as possible.

The wedding was held at the Yeshiva. After evening prayers, the Chupa (wedding canopy) was set up, and the wedding feast was held in the students' dining room. It was very dark outside, so the students obtained a barrel of gasoline and lit it like a huge torch to illuminate the area during the Chupa ceremony and the dancing that followed. From afar it seemed as if the whole camp was aflame, and, in fact, someone alerted the fire engines to come!

Although in the material sense it was a very poor wedding, the exuberant joy and liveliness more than made up for it. As refugees, we were all poverty-stricken. The bride was married in the only dress she possessed! As for me, buying a new suit was out of the question. But German tailors outside the camp could make a suit look like new by turning the material inside-out. It cost me three marks to get that done.

But that wasn't the end of the story. Reb Nissan Nemanov held a Farbrengen and spent a long time talking about...the Yeshiva student who had nothing better to think about before the holy moment of his marriage than to make his suit look new by getting it turned inside out! "Look at what a Yeshiva student puts his mind into..." he said, quoting that as a prime example of the empty pursuits in which a Yeshiva student could steep his mind!

(Incidentally, my father was once asked whether, as a Breslover Chossid, he was agreeable to his son becoming a Lubavitcher. He replied that if I would reach the level of Reb Nissan, he had nothing against it!)

FROM POKING TO LECHVELD

After a while, Rabbi Binyomin Gorodetsky, whom the Previous Rebbe had appointed head of the European office of Lubavitch for rehabilitation of refugees (known as the "Lishka"), informed us – apparently on the Rebbe's directive – that whoever had the required documentation should leave for Paris. Many families left, and Poking's Lubavitcher community dwindled. The heads of the Yeshiva left, to be replaced by others, but eventually the Yeshiva closed.

I wrote to the Previous Rebbe asking where to go. He replied on 10 Iyar, 5709 (1949), that I should go to the Holy Land, adding that I should also try to bring my brother Yisroel – who was still in the Soviet Union – to join me. However, for various reasons, primarily because we did not have the right documents, we were unable to leave for Eretz Yisroel. Meanwhile, both our daughters were born in Germany. Chava was born in Munich, where we stayed until the camp closed. Shterna Sara was born in Augsburg,

Rabbi Shmaryahu Gourary, the Rebbe's son-in-law, visits the DP camp at Poking, Germany

another DP camp in Germany, where we moved afterwards.

Before our daughters were born, we suffered terribly from hunger. At Poking I was still studying at the Yeshiva, for which I received the princely sum of one dollar a week! There was not much a dollar could buy even then. UNRRA (United Nations Relief and Rehabilitation Agency) provided assistance to families with children, but we were not yet entitled to it.

WORKING AS A SHOCHET

I was offered the opportunity to learn Shechita – the

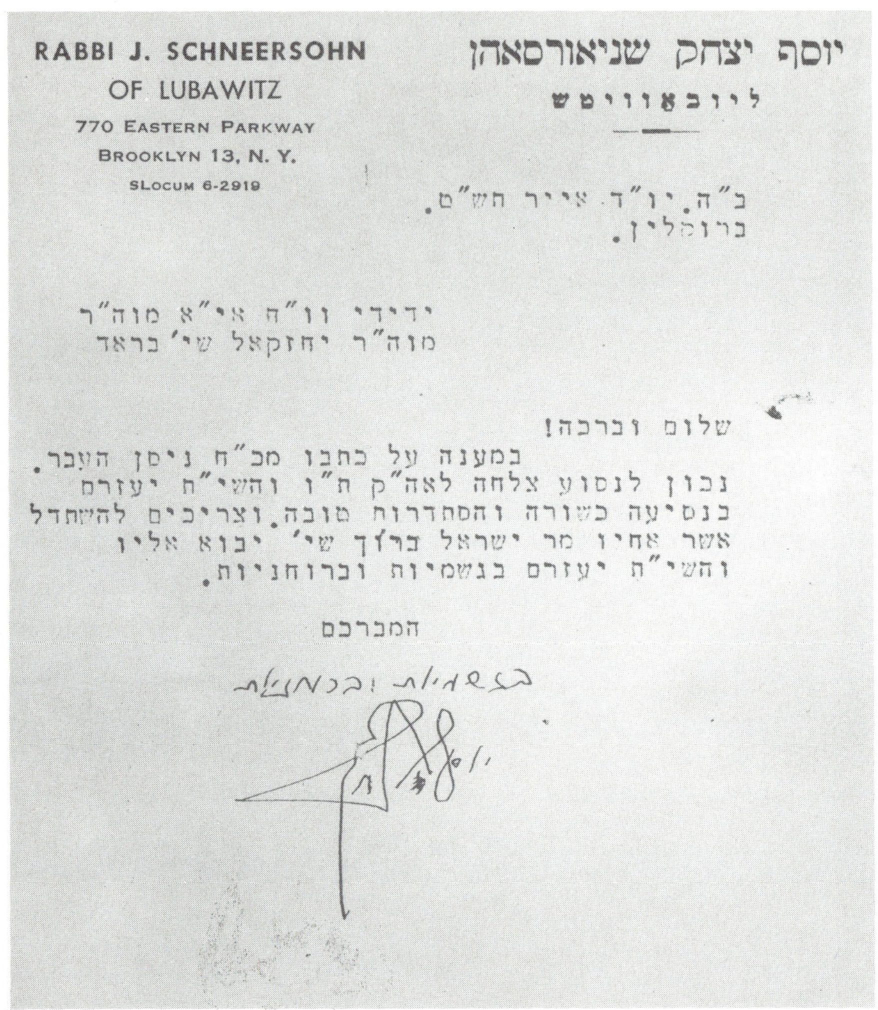

RABBI J. SCHNEERSOHN
OF LUBAWITZ
770 EASTERN PARKWAY
BROOKLYN 13, N. Y.
SLOCUM 6-2919

יוסף יצחק שניאורסאהן
ליובאוויטש

ב"ה. יו"ד. אייר חש"ט.
ברוקלין.

ידידי וו"ח אי"א מוה"ר
מוה"ר יחזקאל שי' בראד

שלום וברכה!

במענה על כתבו מכ"ח ניסן העבר.
נכון לנסוע צלחה לאה"ק ת"ו והשי"ת יעזרם
בנסיעה כשורה והסתדרות טובה. וצריכים להשתדל
אשר אחיו מר ישראל ברוך שי' יבוא אליו
והשי"ת יעזרם בגשמיות וברוחניות.

המברכם

בגשמיות וברוחניות

The Previous Rebbe's letter, dated 10 Iyar, 5709 (1949), instructing me to try and bring my brother out of the USSR to the Holy Land

ritual slaughter of animals. To learn how to slaughter cattle, I traveled several times a week to a slaughterhouse. Often I would leave for my wife the little bread I had managed to obtain, telling her I would be given food at the slaughterhouse – which, of course, was not the case.

In Poking: (R. to L.) Aharon Friedman, Yaakov Katz, the author, Ovadia Schtroks, Elozor Lipsh, Avrohom Roitblat, Yisroel Levin

On a warm day at the Yeshiva. The author is standing in the left of the window. At the far left, sitting, are Rabbi Zalman Shimon Dworkin and Rabbi Eliezer Gurevitch

At a Chassidic Farbrengen: Rabbi Mendel Dubrawski is standing, with the author to his right and Rabbi Nissan Nemanov to his left

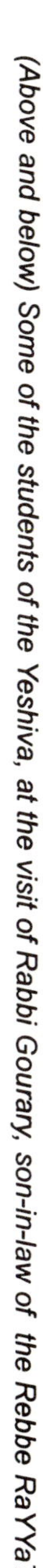

(Above and below) Some of the students of the Yeshiva, at the visit of Rabbi Gourary, son-in-law of the Rebbe RaYYaTz

Our situation improved after I began working as a Shochet. Reb Shmuel Yitzchok Reitzes (a graduate of Tomchei Tmimim in Lubavitch who later lived in Crown Heights, Brooklyn) had been friendly with me while we were still in the Soviet Union. When he left Poking for Paris, he transferred to me his job as the camp's Shochet of fowl.

In Lechveld, too, I became a Shochet for fowl, practicing also at Landsburg, another DP camp about 45 kilometers away that held many Jewish refugees, especially from Hungary, who included many Torah scholars. Between the two camps, I now had ample livelihood.

We settled at Landsburg, from where I left every morning for Lechveld. There I would slaughter until the afternoon, then return to Landsburg, where I would continue until nightfall.

The Rabbi of both camps was Rabbi Yehoshua Moshe Aharonson, known as the "Saniker Rov," who also lived in Landsburg and divided his time between the two camps. He was a prodigious Torah scholar, who wrote a work on the Jerusalem Talmud, among others. (Later he emigrated to the Holy Land, settling in Petach Tikva, where he became one of the most prominent Rabbis, and lived at the end of his life in Emanuel, Samaria. He was a great admirer of the Rebbe RaYYaTz and later of our Rebbe.)

Although he was much older than I, we became very close. He asked me to teach him Shechita, which I did gladly. He was genuinely G-d-fearing and meticulously careful about all details of Kashrus and the other Rabbinical

At a Farbrengen: Reb Yaakov Galinsky, my brother-in-law, is standing on the bench behind me and speaking to the assembled

The author earning his livelihood as a Shochet of fowl

concerns under his jurisdiction.

One example of his Yiras Shomayim (fear of G-d) stands out in my mind: Once, on the day before Yom Kippur, I arrived in Lechveld to find many Jews awaiting me with their chickens for Kapporos (the custom to slaughter a chicken before Yom Kippur as a "substitute" for each individual, in the merit of donating its value for charity). Before starting work, I took my slaughtering knives to the Rabbi – as is customary – to check their sharpness. Rabbi Aharonson found them all satisfactory. After I finished my work, I brought them to him again to check before leaving for Landsburg. This time, too, he found them all satisfactory and wished me "Gmar Chasima Tova," the final greeting before Yom Kippur.

In Landsburg, too, many Jews awaited me with their chickens for Kapporos. After slaughtering for a while, I suddenly looked up to see none other than Rabbi

Aharonson! Immediately I gave him my knife to check, continuing with another one. Again, he found it satisfactory. Later he explained that, although he knew me well as being reliable and had even checked my knives before I left, his conscience had bothered him: Perhaps, because of the unusually heavy workload and pressure of the eve of Yom Kippur, I would fail to check my knife properly!

Meanwhile, the camps were emptying as most refugees left for other lands. We moved to the DP camp of Fernwald, Germany, where I worked again as a Shochet.

(In connection with Fernwald, I am reminded of an incident years later at the Rebbe's famous Farbrengen in Brooklyn on Purim, 5718-1958. As was customary then, I pushed through the crowd to the Rebbe holding a small glass of Mashkeh to ask for a blessing for my family members still in the Soviet Union.

When the Rebbe heard my request, he looked at me and said: "I don't know what's happened to you! I have heard reports about you from the camp at Fernwald, that you used to drink whole cups [of Mashkeh] and it was a 'Mechayeh' [great to see you in the right spirit]! But now you've become a 'Maskil' [intellectual] and you're asking for blessings..."

Those around, gave me a large cup which the Rebbe filled from his own cup and told me to drink, then he filled it again and told me to drink it up and then a third time!)

QUESTION TO THE REBBE

Our big question now was, to where we should emigrate. Although the Rebbe RaYYaTz had told us – and many other

The author inspecting an industrial plant

Lubavitchers – to go to Eretz Yisroel, we were unable to leave at that time. Now we were hearing reports of the poor economic situation there and how those who had already emigrated were experiencing difficult absorption problems.

Rabbi Yisroel Shimon Kalmenson (who later was our Rebbe's Shochet) received a directive from the Previous Rebbe to emigrate to the United States. When he reached Brooklyn, he went to speak to the RaMaSh (as our Rebbe was known before he became Rebbe), who inquired about the economic situation of all Lubavitcher refugee families still in the DP camps. Reb Yisroel Shimon described their problems and mentioned the reports coming from Eretz

Yisroel about the difficult economic situation there.

The RaMaSh promised to report everything to his father-in-law, the Rebbe RaYYaTz, and ask him what they should do. The Rebbe's reply was that although, in general, Chassidim do not ask again after the Rebbe has replied to their question, nevertheless, since the situation had changed, it would be appropriate for each to ask again individually and receive a personal reply.

When we heard this, all the Lubavitchers still at DP camps wrote to the Rebbe asking what to do. Some received an immediate reply to emigrate to the United States. Reb Meir Zarchi, for example, received such a reply dated 7 Shvat, 5710 (1950) – just three days before the passing of the Rebbe RaYYaTz.

However, I received no new reply from the Rebbe RaYYaTz. After his passing, I considered following his original directive of emigrating to Eretz Yisroel, but various obstacles arose.

Eventually our Rebbe, who that year ascended to the leadership of Chabad-Lubavitch, directed me to come to the United States. We started arranging the necessary documentation required for entering the United States and prepared to leave. It took about a year before we could satisfy all the requirements and depart for American shores.

Finally we were ready to leave. After Pesach, 1951, we traveled from Fernwald to the German port of Bremen, where we boarded an American military vessel transporting civil passengers to New York.

CHAPTER THIRTEEN

AMERICA!

CROSSING THE OCEAN

The sea journey to New York was extremely difficult. The boat had originally been a troop transport ship and was not built for the comforts of passenger travel. As a family with tiny children, we suffered terribly during the trip.

Worst, at least at first, was the problem of Kashrus. Of course, we had known in advance that we would be unable to eat from the ship's mess-hall. But we had thought we could survive on bread, vegetables and fruit. However, the morning after we embarked, we went to the kitchen to see how the bread was baked and we were shocked to see that the bread pans were greased with non-kosher shortening.

That left us with no food to eat. We all starved, and our two little daughters became very weak. Other Torah-observant Jews on the ship experienced similar hardship. Non-Jewish passengers even warned us that if we died of hunger, our bodies would have to be cast overboard, for international health regulations prohibited passenger ships from carrying corpses...

The author, after arriving in the United States

We had embarked on a Tuesday. By Friday I was getting desperate to find something on which we could make Kiddush for Shabbos. A Jew on the ship who had traveled from Italy gave me a piece of bread he had brought with him from there, which he guaranteed had not been prepared with fat. On that piece of bread I made Kiddush and it served as our entire Shabbos evening meal.

Clearly this situation could not continue. That Shabbos morning we organized a delegation to the captain to explain our problem and ask his assistance in finding a solution. He listened sympathetically and promised to help, immediately ordering that we be given a pack of Matzos and other acceptable foods from the ship's pantry. On Sunday he arranged for us to be given a sack of potatoes and a new pot, enabling us to cook some food that literally kept us alive during the rest of our trip.

Our ship reached New York two weeks before Shavuos, 1951. We were not allowed to disembark until the U.S.

Department of Immigration interrogated every passenger, which took several hours, especially as we needed a Yiddish interpreter to translate for us. During the interrogation, I was asked whether I had ever been a Communist. I burst out laughing.

"Why are you laughing?" asked the official.

"Because I don't think anyone in all America hates Communism as much as I do!" I replied. He smiled and asked no more questions.

THE REBBE

For so many years I had heard about the concept of a Rebbe from Chassidim who had been present when one of the Rebbes had given a Maamar (Chabad philosophical discourse) or spoken Sichos at a Farbrengen, or who had been in Yechidus (private audience) with one of the Rebbes. Now I was privileged to see the Rebbe myself and experience what Chassidim had seen and felt in the course of the generations.

When we first arrived in New York, we stayed with Reb Yisroel Shimon Kalmenson. On Shavuos, he took me to my first Farbrengen with the Rebbe. The large Shul of 770 Eastern Parkway was not built until the 1960's, and Farbrengens then were held in the small "Zal" (study-hall) upstairs. It was so crowded that the only way I could get in was through the window. I sat astride the window sill with one foot inside and the other out, but felt no discomfort, for I was utterly fascinated by what I saw before me.

The incessant flow, for hours and hours on end, of Sichos

Our Rebbe, soon after ascending to the leadership of Chabad-Lubavitch

on the entire spectrum of Torah subjects - Nigleh, Chassidus and lessons in serving G-d – was amazing to me. Never, neither from great Chabad Chassidim I had known, nor from other Torah scholars I had encountered over the years, had I seen anything remotely comparable to it.

Farbrengens in those days were more informal than in later years, and the Rebbe paid personal attention to almost everyone.

Before leaving home, Reb Yisroel Shimon had told me that in America it is customary for men always to wear a tie, and had given me one to wear. I was not quite sure how to put it on and most probably it did not exactly conform to all the rules of the American dress code. When I followed the example of everyone else and raised my cup of Mashkeh to the Rebbe to wish him "L'chayim," he looked at my tie and smiled: "What? You too have started wearing that 'shmatteh' [rag]? Take it off!" I pulled it off and since then have never been particular about the rules of the American dress code...

Reb Yisroel Shimon Kalmenson, after arriving in the United States

(To illustrate how necessary a tie was

considered in those days: Reb Yehoshua Dubrawski, after arriving in the United States, spent a Shabbos in Detroit, where he addressed the congregation at a Shul. Later one of the congregants told him: "You should know that to us you look like an animal!" Reb Yehoshua was shocked. "Why?" he asked. "Because you're not wearing a tie," came back the reply!)

At our first Yechidus, the Rebbe received us so warmly, with such a beautiful smile, that we were absolutely captivated. His special regard for our little children astonished us. Our older daughter Chava was aged two at the time, and she walked over to the Rebbe's side of the table and stood there next to him. The Rebbe smiled at her and said that she probably wanted to draw a picture. He gave her a pencil, then observed that she needed a paper, too, and gave her one. We were amazed at the Rebbe's fatherly attentiveness to the needs of a little girl.

I asked the Rebbe's advice about finding a source of livelihood, and he suggested looking into possibilities in my profession as a Shochet.

EARLY DIFFICULTIES

We arrived in the United States without belongings, knowing no English, and with no one to help us settle down. We had to start everything from scratch. We rented a room, obtained some furniture and tried to start a new life.

Walking out of the Yechidus, I happened to meet a Lubavitcher who asked if I knew anyone among the recently arrived refugees who was trained as a Shochet, for there was a slaughterhouse in Long Island that needed one twice a week. I saw clearly how the Rebbe's advice was already succeeding. It was only twice a week, and the pay was meager and not really enough to feed my family. But I had nothing else at the time. I sent a note to the Rebbe asking if I should accept, and he agreed.

However, just two days into my new job, I decided to quit:

After the chickens were slaughtered, they were cleaned in a plucking machine. The machine worked with cold water, as required by Jewish law (before the blood is extracted by salt in the koshering process, warm water causes the blood to become absorbed into other parts of the fowl, rendering it non-kosher). As a result the birds did not emerge totally clean of feathers and hair.

Curiously I noticed some women walking out of the slaughterhouse with their chickens as clean as a whistle! When I investigated, I discovered to my horror that the owner kept a pot of boiling water for special customers to dip their chickens in before putting them through the plucking machine, ensuring that they came out immaculate. However, since their blood had not yet been extracted by salting, the boiling water rendered the birds non-kosher!

After coming home, I asked permission to speak to the Rebbe. This was much easier to arrange during those early years of his leadership. I told the Rebbe that I could not work at a slaughterhouse where they deliberately made chickens non-kosher. The Rebbe's face became serious, but he told me not to leave, explaining that while at present some chickens became non-kosher, if I left and a less observant Shochet were hired, the chickens might be slaughtered improperly and all of them would be non-kosher. The Rebbe also advised me to try explaining tactfully to the women how immersing chickens in hot water before salting renders them non-kosher.

With a heavy heart I returned to work. I followed the Rebbe's advice and tactfully told the women about it. Suddenly the owner noticed how women who had always given him their chickens to immerse in the boiling water now asked him not to do so. When he asked why, they replied that the Shochet had said it is forbidden. He made no reply but waited till they left, then walked over to me and told me I was fired: "You're ruining my business!"

Again I was unemployed...

But the Rebbe came to the rescue. He suggested that Reb Sholom Ber Goldschmidt and I go into partnership to open a kosher butcher store. As with all beginnings, it was not easy at first. But gradually we built up a large base of steady customers and eventually made a nice living from it. The Rebbe's blessing accompanied us over all the years.

Unfortunately, during our last three years at the business, we had terrible aggravation from certain individuals, making it impossible to continue. Without elaborating on the problems they caused us, I pray to G-d that the suffering we experienced should atone for and erase our sins, and that those who caused us this suffering should repent to G-d with true Teshuva: "May sins cease from the earth" (Psalms 104:35) – sins but not the sinners themselves (as our Sages say), for they should repent and thereby escape Heavenly retribution.

INVITATION TO THE REBBE

When our oldest son, Yosef Yitzchok, was born in Kislev, 1951, I had a special Yechidus with the Rebbe before the Bris (circumcision), as was then customary. I told the Rebbe that the Bris would be held at our home, and intimated strongly that I would like the Rebbe to be present. He looked at me and asked why it was so important to me.

"Because I want him to grow up to be G-d-fearing," I replied.

The Rebbe asked if I had a phone in my apartment. No, I

The author with his wife and some of their family, in their early years in the United States

replied, but my landlord had one. The Rebbe told me to start the Bris at exactly twelve noon, and to phone his secretary right before to let him know that the Bris would be held momentarily, adding "It's possible to be in both places at once!"

TORAH EDUCATION IN AMERICA

At that time the Yeshivos for school-age children in New York emphasized secular studies to the detriment of Torah study. They seemed far from the pure Torah atmosphere of the Cheder where we immigrants from Russia had studied in our youth, and we were upset at what we considered a compromise with secular culture. But we were told that the very different circumstances in the United States necessitated this and there was no other choice.

When my son Yosef Yitzchok was almost three years old – the traditional age for starting Cheder – the idea of having him study at a Yeshiva where compromise was the norm became more and more unthinkable. One Shabbos, at an informal Chassidic Farbrengen, I drank many "L'chayims" and really let loose. Later I recalled nothing of what I had said, but was told that I had declared tearfully that our great sacrifices for Yiddishkeit in Soviet Russia had not been for the sake of our children later immersing themselves in secular culture: "It wasn't for this that we brought our children out of Russia!"

Many others felt the same, and my outburst made waves. Around that time (on Simchas Torah, 5715-1954), the Rebbe spoke out forcefully on the subject. It was then that

Reb Michoel Teitelbaum, with the Rebbe's powerful encouragement, decided to establish an old-style Chassidic Cheder with a heavy emphasis on Torah studies.

My son Yosef Yitzchok was among the first students of the new Cheder, called Oholei Torah, and experienced all the initial difficulties associated with any beginning. At first the students studied at various small Shuls. Reb Michoel accepted the obligation of raising funds to pay the teachers, and I would often accompany him on his visits to Jewish homes to ask for funds.

Oholei Torah (now also known as Oholei Menachem) has since grown into one of the largest traditional-type Yeshiva systems in the world, with over 1,500 students from nursery until college-level!

THE REBBE'S PERSONAL INTEREST

The Rebbe's extraordinarily warm personal interest in our family members continued over the years.

In 1965, before the mass waves of Soviet Jewish emigration, there were few Soviet citizens, especially younger people, who were fortunate to receive exit permits. Therefore, when we heard that my brother Yisroel had been granted an exit permit, our joy was boundless – it was a true miracle!

Such happy news, I felt, had to be shared immediately with the Rebbe. I stood opposite the Rebbe's door where he would see me when he came out to pray with the congregation.

"I have happy news," I told the Rebbe. "Just now I have

heard that my brother Yisroel has been granted an exit permit!"

The Rebbe's face lit up with his beautiful smile. It was obvious that the news gave him profound personal satisfaction.

As I started to back away, the Rebbe asked me what was happening with my son.

Many months before, my son Yosef Yitzchok had started his last year in Oholei Torah, which was then only an elementary-level Cheder. For the year following, he would be transferring to a high school-level Yeshiva, and I had considered sending him to the Lubavitcher Yeshiva in Brunoy, near Paris, France, where the Rosh Yeshiva was Rabbi Yosef Goldberg. When we asked the Rebbe's advice, he replied that we should first find out about the material conditions there. Later that year, when Rabbi Goldberg visited Crown Heights, he assured me that everything was fine. Now, so long after my original query, the Rebbe was asking me about my son!

I told him what Rabbi Goldberg had said, and again the Rebbe smiled broadly...

MY SIBLINGS AFTER I LEFT THE USSR

When I left home at the age of fourteen, my sister Soroh was still a young child. After the war, when I stayed with my family in Tashkent for a short time, Soroh became so attached to me that, after I left, she fell ill. The doctor advised my parents to bring me back home for a while, but it did not work out.

The author at one of the later Lag B'Omer parades in Brooklyn, New York

When she grew older, Soroh worked to support the whole family. Father, with his long beard and obvious religious appearance, had a hard time finding a job. Soroh, however, found work at a factory where her employer did not mind her staying out on Shabbos. But the other workers were jealous and complained about it. Her boss had no choice but to tell her that, although he liked her work, he could keep her at the job only if she came in on Shabbos, even if she did nothing forbidden by the Torah.

Soroh, however, refused. Even the appearance of going to work on Shabbos, she felt, would seem wrong to others and could have a negative influence on those struggling with the same temptations. Her family was very proud of her brave decision, although they suffered serious deprivation as a result. Soroh's courage in giving up her job made a deep impression upon all the Jews of the city.

Later, Soroh married Reb Yaakov Lepkivker. While still unmarried, he had been caught trying to leave the Soviet Union and was imprisoned for many years. After his release, he settled in Tashkent, where he married my sister. The family emigrated to Israel in 1969 and settled in Bnei Brak.

My sister Reizel's older son is Naftoli Estulin (now a prominent Shaliach of the Rebbe working with Russian-speaking Jews in Los Angeles). When he was old enough to leave home, Reizel took him to Samarkand where there was an opportunity for him to study Torah. She paid a family with whom he stayed and ate meals.

One day Reizel received a telegram that she should come

to take Naftoli home. He had fallen sick and the family was afraid their own children might catch it. Reizel left for Samarkand hoping to find another family with whom he could stay, to enable him to continue his Torah studies. But she could find no one. She had no choice but to bring him home to Tashkent. That day was rainy, but she was so upset that her son might not be able to continue learning Torah that the tears falling from her eyes outnumbered the falling raindrops...

My brother Yisroel's wife, Perela, was from Riga, Latvia - at the other end of the Soviet Union from my parents' home in Tashkent. After the wedding they settled in Riga. However, he could find no job there that allowed him to keep Shabbos. He decided to return alone to Tashkent for a while. There he found a job at which he worked eighteen hours a day! He was so overwhelmed that he used to tie a towel around his waist simply "to hold himself together." Saving all his wages, he returned to Riga with a substantial sum to support himself until, with G-d's help, he found a job there that allowed him to keep Shabbos.

G-d has rewarded him for his self-sacrifice for Shabbos. He moved later to Kfar Chabad, Israel, and he and his wife have a wonderful family of Chassidic children, of whom several are tirelessly involved in the Rebbe's Shlichus work.

IN CONCLUSION

I thank G-d that all my children and grandchildren are following in the path of Torah and Chassidus, for which we sacrificed so much during those dreadful years of Soviet persecution.

May we all be privileged soon to experience the true and complete Redemption, when we will be reunited with our dear Rebbe, who will teach us from the wellsprings of wisdom, the Torah of our righteous Moshiach.

The author and his wife are receiving the Rebbe's Blessing

The author, his wife and children (from right to left): Yosef-Yitzchock, Chave, Yisroel, Shterna-Sara and Sholom-Ber

INDEX OF NAMES

INDEX OF PLACES